Political Spider

Political Spider

An anthology of stories
from *Black Orpheus*
edited by Ulli Beier

AFRICANA PUBLISHING CORPORATION

NEW YORK

Published
in the United States of America 1969
by Africana Publishing Corporation
101 Fifth Avenue
New York, N.Y. 10003

Library of Congress
catalog card no. 79-90296

SBN 8419-0017-5

The editor and publishers would like to
thank Pall Mall Press Ltd for permission
to reproduce the illustrations on pages
1, 71 and 95.

Set in Monotype Fournier and
printed in Great Britain by
Cox & Wyman Ltd
London, Fakenham and Reading

❀ CONTENTS

The Modern World

People

 INTRODUCTION

The stories united in this volume were all published in the magazine *Black Orpheus* in the years 1963 to 1966. For obvious reasons no claim can be made that this selection is comprehensive or even completely representative. Yet the anthology shows some major trends in African writing today.

Nigeria has the largest share in this anthology – simply because more good stories were submitted to the magazine from this country than from elsewhere. North African stories have been included in this volume, even though it has recently been the custom in literary circles to separate Africa north and south of the Sahara. We do not wish to argue the case for treating Africa as a literary unit here. But the juxtaposition of the stories is at least interesting. The French writers from north and south of the Sahara share many themes and problems, and the French language and the Islamic tradition provide two important links between the writers of North Africa and of Senegal or Mali. Three West Indian writers are also included – one has used an African form, another has chosen an African theme.

The concern for African tradition and the use of folkloristic material is strongest in Nigeria. Amos Tutuola is well known among the writers who make use of African folklore. The late D. O. Fagunwa, who influenced Tutuola, is much less well-known, because he wrote in Yoruba. This beautiful translation by Wole Soyinka will give a good impression of Fagunwa's wit and imagination. Bakare Gbadamosi, another Yoruba, is a new name in this field. His subject matter and above all, sense of humour are even closer to the Yoruba tradition. Andrew Salkey, a West Indian, has used the Ghanaian form of Anancy tales to express his own ideas. The title of his story 'Political Spider' was chosen as the title of this book, because it seems to symbolize the efforts of many African writers today; the desire to express new ideas in traditional form and to make use of tradition to analyse the present. By way of contrast Jan Carew of Guyana explores the Indian tradition in his story 'The Third Gift'.

The dignity and ceremony of Islam fascinate both Mohammed Dib, from Algeria, and Ousmane Socé, from Senegal. In 'Zebra', Mouloud Mammeri describes the pious Muslim scholar who can no longer live in the religious seclusion of the old days. Though he understands little of what is happening to him, his life is formed and finally destroyed by political events. Cheikh Amidou Khane, from Senegal describes the conflict between Islam and French culture in 'Ambiguous Adventure', just as Achebe and others have described the conflict between traditional Ibo culture and the modern world. A small extract gives an idea of the kind of argument that goes on in the author's mind. The sophistification of Islam in countries like Algeria and Senegal contrasts startlingly with Nigeaia, where Islam has not so far made any significant contribution to literature.

A great deal of African writing deals with topical themes and the conflicts of modern Africa. The war of liberation is the theme of the Tunisian Henri Krea's story – but it is seen through the eyes of two young children. Luis Bernardo Honwana of Mozambique uses the form of a folktale to talk about racial prejudice. Alex La Guma of South Africa is the meticulous chronicler of violence and suffering in his native land. To him reality is such a powerful thing that he can dispense with a plot in his stories. He needs no beginning and no end. His stories are like snapshots, revealing a terrible moment of truth. Chinua Achebe's story 'The Voter' expresses the author's deep disillusionment with Nigerian politics.

Not all African writing is topical, though. Some of the best writing is simply concerned with people, with their problems and anxieties, their success and their failure. Achebe's Uncle Ben is a man whose life is partly determined by traditional values and myths, even though he is a 'progressive' clerk. Dathorne delights in the description of 'Constable' a charming bum. Bishr Fares, in the most delicate story of this collection, describes the anxieties and nervousness of a young girl who lives in an elated dream world.

The loose division of the stories into four groups should not be taken too seriously: all the categories overlap: 'Political Spider' could be classified under 'Modern World' and Honwana's 'The Hands of the Blacks' could equally come under 'The African Tradition'. The division tries to do no more than provide a possible sequence for school reading.

❋ The African Tradition

Kako ❈ D. O. FAGUNWA

TRANSLATED BY
WOLE SOYINKA

My comrades all, I have beheld the ocean and have known the sea; water holds no further terror for me. My eyes have witnessed much in this world. Yesterday, I told you what scourging I underwent during my second sojourn in the Forest of Four Hundred Gods and I told you how I resolved never again to hunt or set my hand on any arduous task. I must confess this to you, that promise I made, it was a futile thing. I performed yet another deed of a tough nature.

It happened this way – it was in fact the season of the harmattan and I rose late in the morning; too much thinking kept me awake most of the night. I had lately returned from my second hunting adventure and when the women of the town saw in me a new man of wealth, they began to beset my house in thousands and I took them to wife with equal zeal. Many of them did I marry because they were not really interested in my nature. They declared, 'It's your wealth we understand, we have no interest in your character. Even if you wallop us with your gun and bash our heads about with your hunting bag, wed you must.'

But before long, as they began to see my hunter's ways and my riotous temperament which came from a long intimacy with beasts and ghommids of the forest, they began to sneak off one by one, until, on this morning of which I speak, only nine wives were left me. I was chatting with one of them when this hard business on which I was to embark reared its head. This is how it happened:

A king's messenger stepped through my doorway and informed me that the king desired my presence. This was cause enough for amazement and I rose, donned my *dandogo*, my dog's-ears cap, my forty-four bottoms and, fully bedecked, moved on to the king's palace.

No sooner did I come within sight of him than he called out, his cheeks bursting with laughter, 'Akara-ogun', and I in turn replied, 'Kabiyesi, it is indeed I. May God give you a long life.'

Then he sang out to me a second time, 'Akara-ogun' and I answered him, 'Live long, live honoured; we are all children under your fold.'

And yet he cried out to me a third time, 'Akara-ogun' and I replied to him in these words, 'Kabiyesi, it is a veritable man whose name you call. I am indeed Akara-ogun, Ball of Charms; even as my name is, so am I. I am no morsel for the sorcerer, no witch can harm me, no prodigal-with-sacrifice dealer in charms can find a way to touch me.'

The king fell to laughing again and said, 'Seat you on my right.'

When I had made myself quite comfortable he turned to me saying, 'Akara-ogun, my son, I have a mission to request of you, a most important one. And before I even tell you what it is I must ask you, will you perform this task for me?'

I hardly allowed the words out of his mouth before I replied, 'Kabiyesi, this is a very small matter indeed. Wherever it pleases, even there does the wind direct the forest tops; the slave goes simply where his owner orders him – wherever you wish to send me, do so, I must go.'

This promise I made was a most thoughtless one. I had landed smack in the king's trap and he began to address me thus: 'My child, are you aware that there is nothing on earth which surpasses well-being? And do you realize that there is nothing more deserving of honour than serving one's country? These two objectives have greater value than gold or silver, and it is on their account that I have to send you on this errand.

'Before my father died he was fond of telling me about the king of a certain estate which is approached by the same route as leads to the Forest of Four Hundred Gods. The name of this estate is

Mount Langbodo. And he said that the king of the estate had a singular object which he presented to hunters who visited him there. He never mentioned the object by name but he did say that if this *thing* came into the hand of any king, the king's domain would win an abundance of peace and well-being and its fame would resound to every corner upon earth. Because you have journeyed into the Forest of Four Hundred Gods on two occasions, it gives me great joy to summon you today and beg of you from the very depths of my heart not to fail to snatch a brief glimpse of this same king and bring me this *thing* in his possession.'

When the king had spoken these words, I was greatly frightened. For a long time now, I had heard many tales of Mount Langbodo but had never yet encountered anyone who made the journey and returned to tell the tale. Before anyone came into the city he would have to brave the length of the Forest of Four Hundred Gods, and that is only the start of the journey. It can hardly be regarded as a place on earth, because the dwellers of Langbodo hear, in the most distinct notes, the crowing of cocks at the gates of heaven. You can imagine how little I desired any part of such an undertaking, but the promise was made – there was no remedy for going.

'Kabiyesi,' I answered him, 'you are the father of all; and it is truth you reveal when you elders say – the youth can own as rich a wardrobe as he likes, but his rags cannot approach his elder's! I make my obeisance. I learn now that although I boast numerous experiences in my past, yet, in wisdom, I am no match for you. With great cunning you extracted this pledge from me, and whether I wish it or not, I must go. Not that it matters; because it is my own country I serve, go I will. But I crave first a little favour from you. I want you to send a crier round the entire land to summon all fearless hunters such as I and send us together on this quest that my head goes not forth alone to combat death. Nor will this suffice. Send messengers to all the neighbouring villages and homesteads that their bold hunters join us on this mission to Mount Langbodo. If you would only do this, the matter is over; only the going remains.'

The king was made happy by these words from me; immediately he commanded that my wishes be carried out, and within three days, hunters filled the palace courtyard. I looked among these men and I could not find one hunter named Kako. And I knew most surely that he should be part of an expedition of this nature, for a veritable strongman is he.

His history goes like this – his mother, a *lepreet*; his father, a *dewild*. Unfortunately, when their child was born, his skin was almost like a human's and so were his various members. His parents, ghommids both, were having none of this so they abandoned him in a hollow beneath an *ako* tree. A passing hunter discovered him, took him home and reared him. He it was who gave him the name Kako (a foundling by the *ako*). When we were children we played together and it was from this time that I knew what manner of a being he was. When he was twelve he killed a leopard with a matchet and informed no one at home of his exploit. But when the creature had begun to rot, Kako returned to the spot and removed its thigh-bone, turning it into a club, and from then he earned the name of Kako-who-Wields-a-Leopard-Club. Hardly had my father died than his guardian also passed away, and when I went on my first adventure into the Forest of Four Hundred Gods, he turned his feet into the Great Forest. A most evil forest is the Great Forest; its wild beasts are far more numerous than those of the Four Hundred Gods, but the ghommids of the latter exceed that of the Great Forest. At the time of planning this expedition, Kako had not yet returned from the Great Forest and I had to go and seek him there.

I did not arrive at the Forest on the same day as I set out because I was late leaving town. I slept on the way, and about ten o'clock the following morning, I encountered Kako himself. When I saw him, I could not recognize him; he was all covered in palm leaves and I little dreamt that he was getting married to a ghommid on that very day. As soon as he saw me Kako leapt

down from the tree on which he sat, ran towards me and embraced me; there was much rejoicing between us. He told me all
his adventures since he came into the Great Forest and informed
me also that he had heard great things about my own formidable
exploits in the Forest of the Four Hundred Gods. He told me
many, many things but I cannot begin to retell them stage by
stage because such a tale would require a separate book of its own.
And when he had done, I also embarked on the chronicle of my
own harrowing experiences; when I had finished we embraced
each other again and were flooded over with rejoicing, because it
was indeed a meeting of strongmen.

All this while, I did not forget the purpose of my visit, and
after a while I said to him, 'Kako, Wielder of the Leopard Club,
my playmate since our childhood days, will you forbear with me
while I knock off a little proverb ?' And he replied, 'My dear one
Akaraogun, fire away, I'm listening.' So I continued with my
discourse and I said, 'You realize don't you, that if a man's
garments have not seen the last of lice, his finger-nails cannot
have flicked off the last of blood ?' And he said, 'Yes, there is no
falsehood about that.' So I continued and told him, 'Kako, until
we have overcome all obstacles, can we really pause to rest?
There are many goals left for us to conquer, many feats left for us
to accomplish, many marvels waiting for us to perform; our
country still lacks sufficient renown among nations beneath the
sky. Were there no cause to it, a woman would not bear the
name of Kumolu; if there wasn't a good reason behind it, I
wouldn't come so early to seek you out. And the reason is this:
many hunters, many of whom even lack our daring, have girded
themselves in preparation for a journey to Mount Langbodo;
they are going to battle hazards for the prestige of our country,
and when I had given this matter much thought, it came to me
that you ought to go with us. If we do not go, this is a matter of
shame for us, and it would also appear that we only care about
our individual selves and recognize nothing of our country's
needs. And an unworthy thing it is that one forgets one's land,

for let a craft voyage over the oceans and the seas, sooner or later it must head for port; no matter where we triumph in these forests, we must return home some day. My words are, I hope, worthy of your consideration, my friend.'

Let us, unlike the mat unfolding on the ground, cut a long story short. Kako gathered together his possessions, got ready and followed me.

According to the custom of ghommids in the Great Forest, man and woman must live together for seven years before they undergo the ceremonies of a wedding. By then the woman would have given him children and both man and wife would be thoroughly accustomed to each other's ways. If at the end of this period they find each other compatible, they get married – this, in their idiom, is a white wedding. If, however, matters stand otherwise, they take leave of each other with mutual satisfaction, the man to seek a new wife, the woman to hold herself in readiness for another man. It was this form of marriage which accounted for the fact that I found Kako all attired in palm leaves on his wedding day. You would have guessed from this that Kako had lived with his woman for seven years before our reunion in the Great Forest, and it is an amazing fact that throughout his preparations and even up till the moment when he followed me on this wedding day, he had not informed his bride. It was a most unbecoming offence.

But when the woman learnt of his departure, she flew after us, and, on catching up, clung to his feet and spoke thus:

'What can the matter be, my husband? What trouble have I stirred awake? What offence have I committed to warrant this? In what manner have you been aggrieved? Did you discover me with another man? Have I ever spoken in an unseemly manner to you? Have I neglected to show my love sufficiently? Were you told I brawl in public? Did you hear gutter language from my lips? Am I extravagant? Am I vain? Or is it that I am unclean in my habits? Are my manners careless or disrespectful towards you? Am I obstinate towards you? Or is it that I am a failure as

housekeeper? Or have I failed to look after your guests in a
fitting manner? Could it be that I am simply a failure when it
comes to seeing to your comfort? Don't I know how a woman
talks to her husband? Or is it that I have failed to help you in
your own work? What conceivable crime could it be? Tell me,
please tell me, in God's name don't fail to tell me, my Lord, my
husband, my beloved.'

Kako replied and said to her, 'In truth, a woman who knows
all these cautions you have set down could never offend her
husband, and unless I lie in the matter, I must admit that you have
never offended in one of them, not even in the matter of late meals
in which thousands of women are guilty every hour upon earth.
But when a crisis comes, it comes and that is that. At twilight,
hundreds of leaves slumber on the bough; come darkness and
beasts roam the forests in their hundreds – there is a time to
everything; a time to play, a time to fight; a time for tears, a time
even for joy; this is my time for departure, and my going will
yield to nothing. Therefore, go on your way, and I on mine. If
you find another husband, wed him; but do not count on Kako
any more – the son of strangers departs on business of his home –
fare you well.'

On hearing these words of Kako, the woman burst into tears
and entreated him again, but he made no pretence of listening, he
simply grabbed his club, stuck his matchet in his sheath and
walked on briskly as when the office clerk hurries to his place of
work. And when the woman saw that the matter was past help-
ing, she began to speak most piteously in the following words:

'Ah! Is this now my reward from you? When at first you
courted me I refused you, but you turned on the honey tongue
and fooled me until I believed that there lived no man like you. I
gave you my love so selflessly that the fever of love seized me,
that the lunacy of love mounted my head, that love's epilepsy
racked me on your account. I could not eat unless I saw you, I
could not drink unless you were with me; if I wished to go
out you had to come with me, if I heard your voice anywhere I

had to seek you there, and whenever my passion overwhelmed me I would leave my home and wander near yours, talking fast and loud so that you might know I was nearby. You know that I have neither father nor mother, that I have no siblings younger or older; alone you have replaced all these for me. Now when hands have clasped hands and feet slid in step you threaten to abandon me at the very height of day! You wish that I become the laughing stock of all the forest beings who will jeer. 'You were so damned sure; well, tell us, can it be done? Ah, may God judge you guilty, you despoiler of lives!' And she wrapped herself tightly round Kako saying, 'You are going nowhere, not until you find some way to dispose of me.'

Our delay grew longer with the woman's desperate hold, and Kako grew truly angry. His face was transformed and he pulled out his matchet saying, 'Woman of death, witch of a woman seeking to obstruct my path of duty, know you not that before earth destroys the evil-doer, much good has already suffered ruin! Before God adjudges me guilty I shall pass sentence on your guilt.' And having spoken, he slashed her amidriffs, and it lacked only little for the woman to be cloven clean in two; she fell on earth twitching in the final throes of death crying the name of Kako, crying his name into the other world. Great indeed was my terror.

Ajaiyi and the WitchDoctor   ❀   AMOS TUTUOLA

Several years ago, there was an old man who lived in a village. He was a farmer and had one son named, Ajaiyi. This old man was so poor that all of his friends and neighbours believed that he was really created in poverty by his creator. After several years' hard work this poor old man became too old and weary to work in his farm. But Ajaiyi, his only son, took over from him. He was working hard in his old father's farm and by that he was getting sufficient food to feed his father and himself. Ajaiyi worked as hard as he could until he became thirty years old but yet, he and his father's poverty became worse than ever.

Now, one midnight, it came to Ajaiyi's mind to get a wife of his own as all of his friends had. Having thought so within himself for some weeks, he brought this matter before his weary father:

'My father, how can I get money with which to marry a lady as I am old enough now?' Ajaiyi gently asked his father. 'In fact, according to our custom, it is the father's right to pay the dowry of his son's first wife. But now, it is a pity, as you know, that I am so poor that I have not even a halfpenny to give you to pay for the dowry of a lady. I am very sorry indeed, Ajaiyi,' Ajaiyi's father explained quietly with tears. Then Ajaiyi left him in the room and went to the front of the house. He sat on the pavement and wept bitterly.

After a while, it came to Ajaiyi's mind to pawn himself for money. At the same time he went to a wealthy pawnbroker who gave him sufficient money with which he married a beautiful and sensible lady the following week.

A few months after his marriage, his father became seriously ill so that he died within a few days. But unfortunately, Ajaiyi had no money to perform the funeral ceremony of his dead father. Of course as it would have been a great shame to Ajaiyi if he had failed to perform the ceremony, he pawned himself to another pawnbroker who gave him the money to perform the ceremony.

Now, Ajaiyi had pawned himself to two pawnbrokers. He was working for the first from morning till twelve o'clock and for the second from one o'clock till the sun set. But as Ajaiyi had not sufficient time any more to work on his own farm for his and his wife's living, his poverty became more serious. And as everything was still growing from bad to worse everyday, his wife advised him one day:

'Ajaiyi, will you go to the witch doctor and find out the causes of our poverty and find out as well what can stop it.'

Without hesitation, Ajaiyi went to the village witch doctor. He explained to him about his inherited poverty. But with a sharp and merciless voice the witch doctor replied – 'If you want your poverty to stop, you must buy nine rams and nine empty sacks. Having bought all and brought them to your house, you will put each of the rams alive inside each of the empty sacks. Then at midnight, you will carry all to the grave of your father and put all on top of the grave. But to make sure whether your dead father has taken the rams, go back to the grave the following morning. I am quite sure, you will meet only the nine empty sacks on top of the grave and that means your dead father has taken all the rams. But try to bring the empty sacks back to your house and keep them in the room and you will be surprised, in a few days' time, when all are filled up with money by your dead father to find you will be freed from your poverty. But you must come and tell me as soon as you have put the rams on top of the grave!'

When the witch doctor had explained to Ajaiyi what to do before his poverty could be stopped, he thanked him and then left his house.

But as Ajaiyi was returning to his house in the darkness, he began to think in his mind. 'The witch doctor said I had to sacrifice nine rams to my dead father before I could be freed from the poverty! But I believe, I will never be free from this poverty because I have no money to buy even a small cock. How much more do I need for nine rams!'

'What did the witch doctor tell you about our poverty, Ajaiyi?' Ajaiyi's wife hastily asked as he entered the house and he explained to her what the witch doctor told him to do. But as Ajaiyi explained further that he had no money to buy the rams and the empty sacks, his wife said loudly:

'Ah, Ajaiyi, you said you have no money to buy the rams! Are we going to die in this poverty? Better you pawn yourself to the third pawnbroker who will give you the money to buy the rams and the empty sacks!'

'Ah! To pawn myself to the third pawnbroker? But I am afraid if I do so, how can I satisfy the whole of them and who will be working for our own living then?' Ajaiyi asked with great sorrow.

'Never mind about our living, Ajaiyi. I believe if you work hard, you will satisfy all the pawnbrokers!' Ajaiyi's wife advised him strongly.

The following morning, Ajaiyi went to the third pawnbroker who gave him ten pounds. Then he and his wife went to the market with the ten pounds. But unfortunately, the ten pounds were not sufficient to buy the whole nine rams and the nine empty sacks. Having seen this, Ajaiyi was greatly perplexed. He told his wife to let them return home with the money. 'Oh, my husband, don't let us go home with this money otherwise we shall spend it for unnecessary things and yet our poverty will remain as it is. But now, let us buy as many rams and empty sacks as it can buy. Then at midnight, you will carry them to the grave of your father. You will explain before the grave that you will bring the rest as soon as you have money to buy them. And I believe, your father will not refuse to accept them because he knew that he had left you in great poverty before he died.'

Ajaiyi agreed when his wife advised him like that. Then they bought the six rams and the six empty sacks that the ten pounds could buy and they carried them back to the house.

When it was midnight, Ajaiyi put each of the rams inside each of the sacks. He carried them one by one to the grave of his father which was about a half of a mile from the village. Having put all on top of the grave, he explained before it that:

'My father, please take these six rams as the first instalment and I shall bring the other three for you as soon as you help me to get money to buy them.'

Having done all that, Ajaiyi went direct to the witch doctor. He told him that he had carried six rams to the grave. He thanked Ajaiyi with great laughter and then he advised him that he must not keep long before taking the other three to the grave. After that Ajaiyi came back to his house in the darkness. But he had hardly left before the witch doctor and his servants went to the grave and carried the whole six rams to his own house. He killed all for his food and then he gave the empty sacks to his servants to return them to the grave before daybreak.

Early in the morning, Ajaiyi and his wife ran to the grave and both were very happy when they met only the empty sacks on top of the grave for they believed the dead father had taken the rams into his grave. Then with surprise, they carried the empty sacks back to the house. Ajaiyi put them in the room and then he and his wife were expecting the dead father to fill them with the money. But they waited and waited and waited for many months and the sacks were not filled with money and their poverty become even worse. Again all the three pawnbrokers were dragging him here and there for he failed to satisfy any of them. Then he blamed his wife with sorrow: 'I told you in the market that day that we should return home with the money as it was not sufficient to buy all the rams at one time!'

'Ajaiyi, don't let us give up yet, we must try hard. My advice now is to go back to the witch doctor and find out why our poverty is getting even worse than before we sacrificed the six rams to your dead father,' Ajaiyi's wife advised him softly. Again, Ajaiyi ran back to the witch doctor and asked for the reason.

'Ah! your poverty cannot end yet and the sacks in your room cannot be filled with money as you expect until after you have taken the three rams to your dead father!'

The witch doctor frightened Ajaiyi. Without hesitation, Ajaiyi came back to his house and told his wife what the witch doctor had told him.

'What are we going to do next to get money to buy the rams and the empty sacks?' she asked calmly.

'As you know that we have not even one penny in hand, how can we get enough money to buy three rams and sacks! But now, my plan is that when it is midnight, I will visit my father in his grave. I will say to him "You knew that I was in great poverty before you died. But after you died and were buried, you demanded nine rams from me and if I fail to give them to you, I will remain in poverty throughout my lifetime. Of course, I tried my best and brought six for you. But I was surprised to hear from the same witch doctor that you insist on taking the other three rams from me before you would set me free from the poverty which I have inherited from you."'

Ajaiyi explained further to his wife that if his dead father confirmed what the witch doctor had told him to do then he would behead him before he could come out of his grave.

'Ah! Ajaiyi, that is a childish idea. How can you manage to visit your dead father in his grave? Please don't attempt to do that!' His wife was very much afraid.

At midnight, Ajaiyi sharpened his long and heavy matchet. After that he took three empty sacks and went to the grave of his father. Having reached there, he filled two sacks with the earth in such a perfect way that each seemed as if it contained a ram and then he put both on top of the grave. Having done that, he left

the third sack and his matchet on the grave and then he went to
the witch doctor. He told him that he had put the other three
rams on top of the grave. The witch doctor burst into a great
laughter when he heard so from Ajaiyi. He thought that he
would get three rams that night as before. And he was still
laughing when Ajaiyi left him with sorrow and went back to the
grave.

As soon as he reached there, he put the third empty sack nearly
touching the two which he had filled up with the earth. As he held
his long matchet he entered it and cast down in it and then he
was expecting his father to take the three sacks into his grave.
Ajaiyi did not know that it was the witch doctor himself who had
taken the six rams and killed them for food.

After about two hours, the witch doctor and his servants
walked in the darkness to the grave. He ordered his servants to
carry the three sacks to his house. They hardly put them down
before the gods when their master, the witch doctor, began to
loose the sacks in the hope of bringing the rams out and then
returning the empty sacks to the grave before daybreak so that
Ajaiyi might believe that his dead father had taken away the
rams. But he was greatly shocked when he saw the earth in the
first two sacks instead of rams and he hardly loosened the third
when Ajaiyi jumped out suddenly with his long sharp matchet
which was raised above his head.

'Ah! Ajaiyi, you were in the sack as well!' The witch doctor
and his servants defended their heads and faces with hands with
great fear.

Without hesitation, Ajaiyi walked wildly to the witch doctor.
He stood firmly before him as he raised the matchet above head
and said quietly 'Hun: un! my rams in respect of which I had
already pawned myself to the third pawnbroker before I could
get ten pounds and . . . !'

'Oh, let me confess to you now, Ajaiyi! It was not your dead
father who had taken all your rams but I was the right person
who had taken them! I beg you now to forgive me!' the witch

doctor hastily confessed as he began to sweat with fear as Ajaiyi was preparing to matchet him and his servants to death.

'But I believe you are my dead father who has taken my rams therefore you are to set me free from my poverty this midnight!' Ajaiyi shouted loudly as he threatened him with the matchet.

'I am not your dead father at all therefore I have no power to set you free from your poverty,' the witch doctor explained loudly with fear. But Ajaiyi hardly heard him speak like that and he snatched his right hand and asked loudly:

'Tell me the truth! Will you set me free from my poverty this midnight?'

'Only your dead father has the power to set you free from your pov . . .'

But as the witch doctor was still shaking and murmuring with fear his servants rushed against Ajaiyi and he too joined them at the same time. All were just trying to take the matchet from him. Having struggled for a few minutes, Ajaiyi overpowered them when he struck many of them with the matchet. Once more, he snatched the right hand of the witch doctor and began to drag him here and there in the room. And as he shouted for help Ajaiyi closed his mouth with the flat part of his matchet. Having seen how wild Ajaiyi had become that moment, his servants kept quiet as well and they stretched up their hands.

'Certainly, you are my dead father who will set me free from my poverty this midnight!' Ajaiyi roared loudly.

'But Ajaiyi, I am not a dead man but the witch doctor of this village,' the witch doctor murmured with fear especially when he looked around and saw that all of his servants had already escaped outside in fear of their lives.

'Whether you are a dead man or not, I don't mind, but show me where you keep your money!' Ajaiyi shouted and pushed him with the matchet.

The witch doctor walked with fear to the spot where he kept his money in a big pot before one of his fearful gods. He pointed his fingers to the pot. Without hesitation, Ajaiyi put the pot on head and carried it to his house that midnight. When he and his wife counted the money which was in the pot it was more than six hundred pounds. So Ajaiyi and his wife were freed from their poverty that midnight.

 BAKARE GBADAMOSI

The Mouth that commits an Offence must talk itself out of Punishment

In a town called Irandunwo – 'it is pleasant to watch' – there lived a reckless man who was prepared to say absolutely anything. Whenever a bad thing was done, and he knew neither the hand nor the mouth that had committed the offence, he did not mind saying that he had done the thing himself. That is why people called him 'Elenu-obere' that is to say 'sharp mouth'.

Now one day we heard that a certain man had seduced one of the Obás wives and all the royal household was upset. But what do you think Elenu-obere did? He went to the palace to tell people with his mouth that *he* had designed the plan by which the Obás wife had been seduced. His parents warned him not to go round saying foolish things, but they were simply trying to pack corn on the back of a calabash! He told them: 'Nothing will happen to me. As I have not pounded the yam, why should I worry about the pepper in the soup?'

Nevertheless it soon became a matter of 'you look at me and I look at you'. In short, Elenu-obere was taken to court and found guilty of talking rubbish, and he was fined one pound. Elenu-obere was unable to pay and he was to go to prison instead.

Then he hung his head like a sick goat and trouble came and put her child in his arms to rock. Then a kind farmer came along, who said he would lend him the money if only he would work on his farm for four days. Then everybody thought Elenu-obere would take his punishment as a lesson. But they did not reckon with what his mouth could do.

Early next morning the farmer and Elenu-obere set out for the farm. After some time they heard some kind of animal in the bush and Elenu-obere said: 'Surely this is a horse grazing and its left eye is blind.' The farmer thought: there he goes talking nonsense again – after all a nose will never change its shape. And he said to Elenu-obere: 'I don't believe what you say. But if you are right, then I will strike off five shillings from your debt; but if you are wrong, then you will have to give me an extra day's work.'

Soon they came across the animal, and believe it or not, it was a horse that was blind in its left eye. Elenu-obere was happy that his debt had been reduced and they continued on their way.

Elenu-obere was laughing in his belly as they went along – he did not reveal to the farmer that he had noticed the mango-shaped excreta of the horse, and that he had observed that the grass had been chopped only on the right side of the path.

When they reached the farm they did some work before sitting down to eat. As they were filling their bellies the old farmer sighed with satisfaction and Elenu-obere said to him: 'I knew exactly the thought that was in your mind when you sighed'. The farmer thought: this time I have surely caught the fellow, because even if he says the correct thing, I can always deny it. And he sighed again with satisfaction. Immediately Elenu-obere said that he knew the meaning of the second sigh also. The farmer laughed to himself and thought: the putty-nose monkey will always have a white nose and Elenu-obere will always have a stupid mouth. He lit his pipe and sighed for the third time. Now Elenu-obere claimed that he could even explain the meaning of the third sigh. They argued again and Elenu-obere suggested that they should carry their matter before the king. The farmer agreed; he foolishly forgot that it is dangerous to wrestle with a talkative man at midnight. Because even if he was down, he will later say that he was up.

When they stood before the king, Elenu-obere requested that all the royal family should assemble to hear his statements. When they had all come together, he said to the farmer: 'The first thought that came into your mind was: may the almighty God give long life to your king. Your second thought was: may God grant that the king's heir will rule after him. Your third thought was: may this royal house never be replaced by another as long as this town stands'. Immediately the king and all his family and all the chiefs cried 'Amen, amen, amen'. And the poor old farmer was forced to put his lips together and to repeat: 'Amen, amen, amen'.

Thus Elenu-obere was acquitted and absolved of all his labours. The mouth that had put him into trouble had talked him out of it again.

Nevertheless, my friend, it is wiser not to open your mouth too wide. Or can you be sure that your mouth will talk as well as Elenu-obere's?

Political Spider ✾ ANDREW SALKEY

1

Strange as it may seem, the spider's name is Anancy, Brother Anancy in fact, and because he always wore a green coat, his friends, Brother Flea and Sister Leech called him Hope. Of course, Hope was the private name for Anancy and not really a world name at all.

Well, from as early as early morning time, all his personal friends called Anancy Hope which, as you know, is a green thing, eternal and all that; and it's for that same reason that a whole heap of bangarangs was to happen to them.

You think you understand the position now?

Now, as a matter of habit, most people can't put out the white light from their minds when they remember that particular morning time, bright like Big Massa candlelight, when Brother Flea and Sister Leech sat down like double statues, holding on and waiting for Anancy to come and talk his talk about settling all the botheration of the jobless spiders, fleas and leeches.

What an Anancy morning it was!

2

The faces of the spiders, fleas and leeches had plenty of uneasiness pricked all over them, like tattoo marks. The spiders, fleas and leeches sat down quiet and strong and ancient like the Boss Man heraldics in the Manor House on North Hill. Everybody was listening to the silence which was yellow like a sort of sickness. Still and all though, yellow silence is a good thing for the thinking out of worries and problems, and it's a hard silence to keep, hard to keep like fast-time in the wilderness. And that was why, like a piece of tight-stretch elastic just begging to snap in two, the quiet started to break up right there and then.

Talk-time. Listen to what one short-arse flea is saying to his long-foot flea friend: 'I bet you anything that Anancy going be late. Funny sort of spider man that. He always doing all sorts of top hat things as if he face to face with society people. I think he got a bad buckra complex, you know.'

Long-foot flea now: 'Complaining can't make rain come. If you talk bad 'bout Anancy, it don't mean to say that we going get job and eat better.'

Short-arse: 'But he always promoting himself up to the people on North Hill and I sure this action is a disease that catching; it must be a disease, this eye-signalling and talking with those who come from a different class of ideas and life.'

Hear the answer: 'I not backing down, but you got a point there. That is our trouble. Always, always, Anancy out of reach when we need him bad. He is one green coat spider who born to rub up against high wall and talk deep talk with a heap of strange people. Sometimes I think that Anancy is too much of a political spider for his own spider good and for our own.'

Short-arse again: 'I don't mind if Anancy want to rub green coat 'gainst politics and things like that, because, to tell you the honest truth, the politics business need some green rub off on it. What worrying me is that Anancy getting too deep into the life of those well-off people. You know what I mean by that?'

Long-foot: 'True. Anancy born inquisitive. He born with a travelling eye from a long time back. But as you know, it is an equal easy thing for spider web to get tangle-up with all sorts of outside foolishness.'

Short: 'And when that is that, a spider can find himself well on the way to the overseas thing called compromise, and bad starvation and dark eye might follow, because a spider can't catch no dinner at all with compromise burden dragging him down.'

Just as this talking was building up into a mountain of giant statement and giant sighing and giant breathing, one old-time spider, with three spangles missing on his right side, decided to chip in and add some old-time wisdom. Listen to him talking: 'You young people, with your egg shell still wet, really love to beat up your gum like drum skin rolling at John Connu time, eh! No John Connu dance, you know. You always broadcasting your doubt like red peas on top of ready brown dirt. Grow, you want your doubt to grow like plantation, yes?'

Long and Short stared at him and blinked.

Old-time spider: 'You all want to cause big muster and botheration 'mongst the population down here, eh? Well, let me tell you something you don't know. You know that Anancy is Hope is a spider is a fighter for everybody. You know that Anancy is a spider is Hope is a green thing.'

Long and Short nodded like wise young fleas.

'Well, now,' Old continued, 'if that is so, true and honest, where in the name of boundaries and limits, from Guyana all the way up to Jamaica, do you expect Hope to spend his time and energy, except on high places where he can put telescope on our wants and suffering?'

Not a word from Long and Short.

After that piece of wisdom-talking, a crowd began to gather round them.

Old, not too slow in coming forward, or for that matter, not too shy to hold on to the spot, decided to add one more difficult statement to his pretty speech: 'The best place for Hope is 'mongst the enemy. A spider got to know how the land looking outside the home web. Living with the opposition is correct politics.'

The shape of the crowd was moving busy like ants in a fat nest. Everybody was shifting brisk and electric-like. All sorts of mad barber shop talk started to go on with plenty body-fire and hand-crackling. Spiders and fleas and leeches talked about deep high-class subjects like the quality of Hope and the everlasting example of patience. One light-skinned spider got up and began to spread himself all broad and useful as if he was some sort of a new asphalt road or something, and he let loose plenty words and lots of pictures in the air with his spangle-hands; but if you actually stopped and added up all the things he was talking about, you would get approximate total nothing. According to some spiders in the know, he was in training as a Park lawyer; so don't mind him.

Then sudden like a shock, like *ackee* without salt fish or vicky verky, Anancy breezed into the crowd and began to fix his papers and his face like he was about to talk House of Representatives talk at crisis-time, like out of many one. He stood up and cleared his throat and delivered in his usual Tate and Lyle voice. This is a voice he always put on for the benefit of the crowd as if he was talking to a cane-piece gang.

Hear him now: 'Morning, my brothers and sisters! I have, here, with me, a master plan which will bring us a demi-john of contentment of mind, if only you all obey me to the z of it.'

Everybody hung on to the z and wondered what would come before it.

'Countrymen!' Anancy went on, cool as cubes. 'According to my right-hand members, all two of them, Brother Flea and Sister Leech, there is no world without rain. They say work scarce and the fields empty like baby belly six o'clock in the morning.'

The crowd of spiders, fleas and leeches applauded a small bomb and smiled confidence all over the place.

'*All this!*' Anancy roared. 'All this is going on, while in other parts, wallets and hand-bags bulging with prosperity like school-boy back pocket with broken plate, string, marble, cotton reel and so.'

He chuckled a pure parliamentary chuckle. Then he paused, stamped his spangles for total attention, and got it. He chuckled again. Then suddenly he looked like a great leader about to do a Moses.

This is it: 'Well, brothers and sisters! Since other people bellies bursting with good imported food, and you, my very own people, starving and crying out for pity, home-made bread and butter, I going tell you what to do.'

Pointing towards North Hill, Anancy made an order, in a torrent voice: 'All fleas must take up easy residence in all the fat dogs straying up yonder; all leeches must make houses in the soft under-belly of the horses and cows heeling the uplands; and all spiders must hang from the mahogany rafters and beams holding up the great houses on North Hill.'

The direction Anancy pointed to was definitely North Hill. And Hope which is green which is Anancy just simply can't be wrong no how.

His second-to-last final words: 'Move up! All of you must move up in life! Feet first, soul after!'

And so, Sister Leech fixed a committee in a flash. She got Brother Flea to head it. She also brought in short-arse flea, long-foot flea and old-time spider to serve. And everybody held a quick sale to the border people and started to climb the hill to better life. Some called it the road to contentment; some said it was the way from plantation wages up to the stars, from Frome to North Hill.

Spiders, fleas and leeches travelled for days and nights, adding up to half a mango season, and they were travelling and obeying Anancy's orders to the ʒ.

Z was: *All spiders, fleas and leeches must throw away a little of their old belongings after every fifty yards of the journey until all their belongings have been disposed of. Secondly, after every additional yard or so, a slight hole must be dug to open the land to the coming rains. Thirdly, the journey to North Hill must be done in a slow walk; hurrying is never wise or profitable when Hope is*

*handling affairs. Fourthly, the highest wall of walls must be built
after crossing into the lands of the North Hill.*

But that was not all. Anancy even had Brother Flea and Sister
Leech speaking in his voice and in his words. Brother Flea:
'The rains won't fall until we all return from North Hill con-
tended and fat. And when we return, the land we put holes into
will be ready to meet us half-way with bags of blessing. And
remember, the heavenly mystery of rain, the special bonus will
depend on our faithful co-operation on the land.'

Sister Leech: 'You can't fool the rain, and you can't fool the
times we live in. Everything is up to us to meet the rain half-
way.'

The journey lasted fifty more days and nights.

By this time, the land was full of holes, and all over the place,
there were piles of belongings spread out like Monday washing in
a giant back yard. Old-time spider, in all his wisdom, imagined
that the items left behind were more like dead things: Willy
pennies, cycle-sports betting slips, bottle stoppers and a mixture of smalls which had cute value if you knew where to take
them.

Well, now, everybody made the crossing and dropped into the
grounds of North Hill like Christmas pudding, sweet and heavy.
Big 'fraid and shyness held on to the new arrivals.

North Hill was quiet as Moses' baby bottom in bulrush.

And so, every single man Jack began to build the highest wall.
Movement was noise was organized construction going on.
Quick and brisk, Babel broke out, and the wall going up faster
than factory smoke.

3

Anancy, watching a Nelson watch a distance away, grinned a
jaw-to-jaw grin. His spider eyes were sea-beacons, bright and
full of messages from the coast side of the brain. Click! He stood
up on a parapet and shouted: 'My people! With you! Wants

going satisfied now. Bellies going fill up. Eyes done watering. Opportunity. Progress. No more Up-Class versus Down-Class. New ground before you. But careful one thing!'

Anancy stopped short. He liked doing that sort of Question Time pausing for effect. He hunched his shoulders, and his green coat wrinkled and formed a miracle of folds. He narrowed his eyes and cleared his throat. Hear him: 'Nobody must venture away from North Hill unless the others ready to move back to the Old Country. All must move as a group, like family. Stick together and work for the V.C.G.'

Brother Flea raised his trowel and said: 'The Very Common Good!'

Anancy nodded. Then he shifted his spangles and rubbed his green coat as if he loved it and himself all in one go.

Everybody looked up at Anancy as a sort of celebration column come to life on the parapet, as if he was the coming rain. there was no rain coming at all. It was only Anancy coming up with: 'North Hill is yours. One for all. All for one. Out of many one.'

Stamping spiders legs, clapping leech mouths and hissing flea gills made plenty Park bench commotion. And Anancy stood steady like a big time trans-Atlantic planner and took all the congratulation noise as if he had been born to it, as if he had organized it in his sleep, cool and easy. His face was so steady that it looked museum important. Then he waved for silence and pointed to his green coat. This now: 'Hold back the merry-merry and ponder this. Final words make history. Work hard and grab. All leave together. My name is Anancy is a spider is Hope is a green thing!'

4

After he had bowed out all spruce up and down and smiling and waving off the scene, he coiled himself away tight into a ball and shot back to the land in the Old Country.

Time, and rain poured and lashed, as was natural. The land sprang up like a young something. It belched plenty benediction in vegetables and fruits and things yellow, green and red. The flat earth began to look big, and in next to no time at all, it was mothering peas and yams and cocoa and bananas and sugar cane. Trees and streams were botanical with a vengeance, and breezes blew calmness everywhere, and all the hard-to-get richness of Up came down to the Old Country.

But Anancy, cunning spider he is, loved the aloneness when all the sweetness was happening to the land, and he reaped every drop in sight. Then he bagged the old belongings of the spiders, fleas and leeches, and made a brazen sale to Brother Tacuma, the world-famous travelling merchant with a fitting nose for large deals. And right after that, Anancy disappeared for the last time from the Old Country.

If you had been there at the time and looked at the land after Anancy had dusted it, you would have seen a proper barren Bible country. Not a thing was left behind, not a tree with fruit, not a touch of goodness, not a piece of yam or cocoa or sugar cane. As a matter of story, the only thing that was left was silence and sales echo.

5

Slap bang, and back to North Hill. Hold on to your brush when I tell you that all the spiders, fleas and leeches were, by now, even more poverty-stricken than before the trek. This was so, because they found no fat dogs, no soft horses and cows, no mahogany rafters, no beams.

Season of breeze-blow. Season of sun-hot. On and on like so. And the numbers dropped from three million to sixty-three only. Some settled for suicide; some died from hungry belly and dark eye; some were crippled flat on the ground when they tried to scale the highest wall they had built themselves; and some cried and died from worry-head. But, as with the Ark and loud bangs, there were the survivors: Brother Flea and Sister Leech. They were humping hard-earned experience around with them and still waiting like green fruit for ripening.

'So, short-arse and long-foot kick the bucket, eh?' Brother Flea said.

'And old-time spider, too,' Sister Leech said.

'And that other one,' Brother Flea hinted. 'Done it again, sure as sin.'

'Who that?' Sister Leech asked.

'Who but Anancy.'

'You know something, Brother Flea? I think that all this is a Job lesson. Anancy teaching us a deep something 'bout ourselves and 'bout our struggle on the land in the Old Country. That's what.'

'Sister Leech, I was thinking, too. Green is a funny colour.'

'Green, Brother Flea?' She was drifting. She really hadn't heard Brother Flea's words at all. Sudden *wappen-bappen!* And she screamed as if a low belly pain caught up with her.

A pause.

'Lord!' she shouted. 'Look, a pipe!'

The stand-pipe in front of them was old and twisted. It dripped rhythm.

Brother Flea and Sister Leech took foot and walked over to it and listened to the music coming 'drip-drip-drip-drip', and Brother Flea looked wide at Sister Leech, because the music was saying something he had heard somewhere before.

Brother Flea and Sister Leech started to laugh quiet-like. And the music talked to them. Then both they and the music got louder and louder, and Brother Flea and Sister laughed a pair of store-bought bellows, on and on until you'd think they'd burst open like two over-ripe jackfruit. The laughing was stronger than Samson roaring, and steady as a river running glass to the sea.

6

And if you walk near to your own stand-pipe, you'll hear the same music talking to you. And it would be saying the same everywhere: '*Is Anancy is a spider is Hope is a green thing is politics is Anancy is a spider is Hope is a green thing is politics is Anancy is Anancy is Anancy!*'

The Third Gift ❀ JAN CAREW

In the last days of the prophet Amalivaca he led his people to the foot of a high mountain. Now these savannah people were called the Jubahos (the wanderers) and they were an itchy-footed people – they always like to live in the open llanos where there was nothing but sky and tall grass 'round them and wan't little trouble the ole prophet had to make the Jubahos settle down in a place where every time a man turn round he had a mountain blocking his view. But it wasn't Amalivaca preachifying that influence the Jubahos so much as hungriness and drought, 'cause year in, year out, the sun turn vampire and dry up the savannah, parch up the long grass, dizzy up the horizon with heat-haze, 'till a clump of grass was worth the price of a wild horse. So the Jubahos pick up their few belongings and follow Amalivaca and when they reach the flat, green lands that stretch out at the foot of the mountain, weariness was killing them. People ask:

'Is what this mountain call, Amalivaca?' and the prophet say. 'Neither this place nor the mountain en't got no name so we will call the mountain, Nameless.' And is so Nameless Mountain get a name. Now this mountain thrust up so high that nobody couldn't see the peak for all the mist that was hugging it close but the foot of Nameless Mountain was green and day and night you could hear the water tumbling down the mountainside. Well once the Jubahos start to settle in and shake off the strangeness of the place, wasn't long before Mantop, Death's messenger-boy, was crouching in the moonlight shadows to ambush old man Amalivaca. The night Mantop howl outside the prophet's benab the old man gather the people 'round him and say:

'I lead all you far and now the time come to set out for the forest of the long night. Mantop, Death's messenger-boy waiting for me outside and en't much time lef' before I must harness up my wareshi and go....'

'No, Prophet, no!' the people shout, 'Is how we goin' live without you?'

'Listen to what I have to tell, my face beat 'gainst plenty years already and time running out on me! All you must chose a new Prophet from 'mongst you, all the strongmen must set out up Nameless Mountain and the one that climb the most high and bring back a gift of the wonders that he see, *he* all you must make prophet...'

So Amalivaca start out for the forest of the long night and when day broke even the wind was heavy with lamentation and all the strong men set out up the mountain like the prophet did say – up past the orchids and simitu vines on the moss face of rocks, up to where wild mango does stripe the slope with white and green, up to where secret springs does gurgle into rivers, up and up they climb 'till all they could hear was wind in stranger trees.

A whole day pass and wasn't 'till sun was yellowing and tinamous start to warble and flute that one strongman come back weary and sleepy like mud and the others follow him dragging they feet – but the one that climb the most high come running down holding something in his hand, high above his head, he was running deer-speed and he didn't stop 'till he reach a clearing and the folks gather 'round him.

'Show us what you bring!' they keep shouting and the man say:

'Come near and see, this is what I bring – eye never see and hand never feel thing like this,' and he open his hand and the women hold they head in wonder.

'Look at the curve of it and the way it catching light all over it! Lawd, is a wondrous thing, eh!'

And this thing that the man bring to show was a stone shape jus' right to fit inside a man's hand and when it catch the light it

had all the colours of the mountain orchids and more and when
he hold it up even them who envy him start to heap praise on his
head like fire.

'But is what message you bring with the stone, Prophetman?'
somebody ask.

'This stone is the gift of work,' he say, and the minute he say it
the whole gathering has visions of plough-blades and axe-blades,
knives and cutlasses and corn and cassava growing more plentiful
than grass.

Now because this young man bring the gift of work, the folks
make him prophet and he rule long and the tribe multiply and the
people push the memory of hungriness far from them.

But came the time when this prophet had to follow the trail that
Amalivaca took to the forest of the long night, and the lamentation weigh heavy on the heart of them he left behind.

So for the second time all the strongmen of the tribe wait for
the sun at fore-day-morning and set out up Nameless Mountain.
And the man who climb the highest this time come down the
mountain trail softly-softly 'cause he had something that could
break easy if he run too fast and again the folks gather 'round
him and this time they didn't have to ask what he bring 'cause
high above his head he was holding a flower. And nobody never
see a flower so beautiful with the petals curve up so and the colour
of it bright so. And the new prophet didn't have to tell the story
of this gift 'cause all who eye light on it know that it was the gift
of beauty.

And this prophet rule through many moons. And, Lord! the
village became a place to see! Every hut-door had flower patterns
carved on it, the girls start to wear wild flowers in their hair, and
every canoe that go up and down the river had a flower carve out
of purpleheart wood in the prow. Yes, was a joy to live in the
village then. But still everybody wasn't satisfied – they all had
work and beauty and yet they wanted more and some even start
mutter that they were thinking 'bout searching for another land
down river and 'way across the plains. So when Mantop came

for the second prophet and take him 'way to the forest of the long night, everybody knew that the new prophet would have to bring a powerfu' gift from the mountain to hold the tribe together.

So the strongmen set out up Nameless Mountain for the third time. And 'mongst them was a dreaming sad-faced young man who always used to look like he had a mountain of thinking on top of his head. Came night time and the fireflies start winking over the cassava fields and everybody else came back except that dreaming young man. And the folks ask:

'Is where that young man? Is why he en't come back yet? We 'fraid for he!'

And the weary ones who return say:

'We see him climb up to the mist and he keep going up and up and none of us had the strength to follow him.'

Night time come and go and the young man didn't come down from the Nameless Mountain and they post look-outs to watch for him – the women take turns by the river bank and the young men on the mountain slope. Sun and Moon lengthen many shadows and still the young man didn't come back. And there was plenty discussion about the young man who go his lonesome way up the mountain.

'He will come back with a powerful gift to ease sorrow in our heart,' they all say.

One morning bright with dew and singing birds an old woman was beating clothes with her paddle by the riverside and singing, all of a sudden she stop and shout:

'I see something coming down the mountain!'

Everybody lef' what they was doing, and they all raise their eyes up to the mountain and watch and wait. And soon it was clear for all to see.

The man come running down, parting the long grass, leaping from rock to rock. And he was holding his hand high, clenching his fist and coming like a tiger was behind him. He reach the riverside and burst across the cassava fields trampling the young plants down. And when he reach the village he wouldn't stop.

'Aye, aye, brother, you home now, man! We was waiting for you 'till our hearts were loaded with the waiting!' But the man wouldn't stop. He keep on running.

'Stop! Stop! You home, man!' But he would 'ave run right through the village and away if he didn't trip up on a piece of firewood and fall down. And he lie down on a patch of young grass blowing like his chest-box wanted to burst, with his hand clench tight.

'Is what you bring, brother? Talk to we! Is what you see over the mist on Nameless Mountain?'

The man didn't have words to answer, he just lie heaving and blowing 'till an old woman bring kuru oil and anoint him. The men folk couldn't wait to see what he had in his hand so they pry his fingers open, and when the hand was opened for all to see the people standing 'round gasp . . . 'cause the hand was empty. Was then that the young man find his tongue and say:

'I got up to the mist and over and above it and I didn't know how long it take 'cause past the mist was a brightness that blind my eyes and came a time when all I felt was a soft carpet under my feet and when I breathed in the mountain air it was like drawing knife blades up my nose. And when my sight came back I found myself right up at the mountain top. . .'

'Lord you must 'ave seen the whole world from there, brother!'

'Yes and while I stand up there a soft white thing like rain start to fall . . . and yet it wasn't rain 'cause it fall slow like a leaf when there is no wind . . . it fall and flutter and spin and some of it settle on my head and my shoulders and I reach out my hands to catch some of it . . . and when I hold it in my hand one minute it was like fire and next minute it was cold like a mountain pool . . . so I catch a handful of it and press it hard in my hand. And I feel Wind fluting in my bones and I set out on my way back home – and all the time I was feeling this thing in my hand – and down the mountain side I ran. Sun hide himself from me when I was in the mist, and leap out at me again when I burst through and come to the green of the mountainside, and the wind was cool on my face and the whole plain and savannah stretch before me. And the further down the mountain I come the less of this thing I had in my hand, 'till when I reach by the river was only memory I had in my hand.'

And this man whose name was Jymara become prophet of the Jubaho people 'cause he bring the best gift of all . . . the gift of imagination, of fantasy, of faith. And Jymara rule his people for all time.

❋ The Islamic World

A Beautiful Wedding   MOHAMMED DIB

Three announcers went from house to house and a public bell ringer went through the town to proclaim the wedding.

Aini and her three children Aouicha, Omar and Meriem were to spend the night with Aunt Hasna. The boy refused at first to do so. How much had been spoken about this wedding! In Omar's imagination this belonged to those events of which everybody talked wildly but which never took place. It seemed too big and beautiful a plan.

And now Aouicha returned from over there with a list of all the dishes that were being prepared. Aini and the little ones who were listening to her could hardly believe their ears. Aouicha swore to it; after all she knew the sort of thing that was being offered at distinguished weddings!

But that they were among the invitees themselves confused them completely. The meaning of this wedding was suddenly driven home to them.

All four of them were silent for a moment. Even Aouicha looked surprised. 'That is not all,' said Aini suddenly.

For a few moments she too had been enraptured by this dream: vehemently she removed the luminous vision.

'That is not all, my children. Listen well to what your mother is telling you; try of the dishes that will be offered to you there, but only take a little. Do you understand? Only with the finger-tips. I shall be watching you.'

The children seemed sad. They looked at their mother critically.

Aini whispered in an angry tone: 'I do not want people to say that my children are starving . . . that we go to this wedding because of the food. Even if we are poor we must keep up our dignity.'

Omar thought: 'For people like us life means eating. And the pleasure of life is the pleasure of eating.' His mother's words were humming in his head.

'A moderate pride is necessary in a life like ours,' she used to say. 'Even if one is only a cobbler or a weaver one has to carry one's head high as if one were descended from the Rothschilds.'

At all important ceremonies like weddings and religious feasts the children must always be present. In our town it is unimaginable that the children will not play an important part when anything is happening. At the entrance to the quarter the little street was barred by a group of boys and girls. Some of them were wearing festive clothes; these were as usual as green trees in winter. The others were like Omar and had decorated themselves in their own fashion.

They were chasing each other, shrieking as loud as they could. The smallest ones were crying.

It was really the unusual event that one expected, that one looked forward to. There was an intoxicating activity, an atmosphere of joy.

The guests were arriving, and assembled at the inner part of the house. The announcement of a wedding is always an exciting event for the women. Whenever a woman has been invited to a wedding, she asks permission from her husband to take part. Immediately the head of the family hides himself behind a threatening silence. But finally he gives in. In fact he cannot really refuse this. Happier than ever, the woman dresses up in her most beautiful finery.

It happens, and not infrequently, that more guests arrive than were expected according to the invitations.

The first guests filled a room, and new ones joined them continuously lining up along the walls. They were all devouring the bride with their eyes. She was sitting on a chair in a ceremonious pose. The gold veil that covered her face completely did not move. Custom did not permit her to speak. But it might happen that she moved just a little bit. In this case she was expected to regain her complete immobility quickly.

Whatever the character of a bride, on her wedding she shows nothing of it. The bride one saw here was unattainable. Tradition was much too strong – it was of impressive grandeur – for the bride even to move an eyelid. The guests were touched by this spectacle.

At this moment the bride concentrated on herself all the serenity that was in the air. Everybody talked in a low voice, although this was a great effort for the women. Gradually the conversation became livelier; a subdued murmur rose from one end of the wide room to the other. The women were filled with gentle seriousness and graceful reverence.

'Do not forget, my dear,' said one of the women to another, 'that men of today like to have a wife who knows how to dress and who can bear them company.'

The answer came promptly.

'Her dowry is so large that she can adorn herself for the next ten years.' And she added proudly: 'You will see this dowry immediately.'

Another one, apparently one of the husband's relatives, said contemptuously: 'It will be like any other dowry.'

The other replied, red and trembling: 'No, my little one, it is not like all the others. All who have seen it stood there open-mouthed. Everybody knows what we spent on it. . . .'

An old grandmother tried to appease them: 'This is a holy day . . . let there be peace in this house.'

These words seemed to soothe the opposing views and the discussion ended.

Then the children arrived. They pushed themselves into the house by pinching the arms and calves of those who stood in their way. They arrived almost creeping and lined up in front of the bride. Her splendour fascinated them. Omar wanted to fill his heart with this image. She was covered with silvery and shiny cloth that reached down to her feet. Calm and erect she sat on her chair without a tremble. Only her breath moved her breast. A pointed hood, gold-embroidered and studded with glistening sequins, rose above her forehead. The veil that covered her face was fastened to the point of the hood and fell down to her shoulders. Before this faceless idol Omar was seized with strange excitement.

The face was shown only to certain women. And a female relative had to be there to unveil it. The bride remained immobile, as if she had fallen into a deep sleep. When the veil was lifted, her motionless face and her lowered eyelids appeared illuminated by shimmering silk and precious stones. Mother of pearl and rose colour lay on her brow, her lips, her cheeks. The white of her arms, that one could observe at ease, was glimmering beneath her clothes like snow. Her ringed hands rested on her knees and showed a network painted with henna that reached up to the elbows. The palms of her hands and her finger-nails were dyed. How pure and indifferent her attitude! One could have thought that she took no interest in the splendour that was displayed on her, around her and for her.

Suddenly excitement arose.

'Turn them out, those rascals!'

The children had to leave the room. The women left their places and scolded the children and slapped faces or punched their ribs until they had all gone. Screaming much louder than the slaps warranted, they left in tremendous confusion, curses on their lips. . . .

They spread out in the courtyard. But other women were expecting them there, and chased them away.

The children amused themselves by chasing each other in the general confusion. In the meantime the guests were streaming in. The noise, the crowd, the varied dresses, the confusion of

colours, were quite intoxicating; and nobody really knew what
wild, bubbling fair was beginning to unfold.

A girl proposed: 'Let's play wedding day!'

The boys remained indifferent; so the girls repeated: 'We'll
play wedding day!' They were all shouting: 'To the wedding, to
the wedding!'

They were surrounding the boys, who, pressed from all sides,
finally gave in.

Omar showed his aunt's room. He knew how to get there.
He climbed up the stairs to the first story, and gave a sign to
those who followed. He pushed up the hook of the shutter;
then he climbed up and jumped into the room, followed by the
rest.

When they were all there, they were hiding under the huge bed
of aunt Hasna, an incredibly high bed from old times; the children
did not touch it with their heads. They formed a circle. Yasmina
was chosen to be the bride. She accepted her role, without saying
a word. Her tender, oval face looked serious. She had long,
smooth hair, and green eyes. The bridegroom was a curly-haired,
lively boy. The girl sat down quietly in front of him, and waited.
The children asked her to shut her eyes. A veil, which they had
taken from Aunt Hasna's cupboard, was spread over her. Then
they were all looking at each other. At last the bridegroom took a
decision. He wetted his finger with spittle and touched Yasmina's
body.

There was a confusion of voices in the house. Odours of stew
and fried meat rose from the ground floor. When the youngsters
noticed these smells, they could not contain themselves any
longer, and they all jumped out of the window again.

The *meidas*, small round tables had been set up in the yard.
The guests helped themselves to large pieces of mutton that were
swimming in saffron sauce. Oh, all that meat! In addition, cuscus
was served, decorated with dates and sliced eggs. Aunt Hasna had
prepared the feast well.

Some women were eating with their ten fingers. The red of

their lips was melting in the fat that covered their mouths. But the elegant ladies next to them behaved like tailor's dummies.

The children were mixing freely with all the groups, snatching what they could get, remains of meat and bread. They stepped aside a little and swallowed the remains which they had pinched as quickly as possible. They were surrounded by fluttering doves that were trying to pick the crumbs.

Aunt Hasna, leaning forward, had her eyes everywhere. With her severe voice she shouted orders to the cooks and then she welcomed the arriving women. Her broad hips were adorned with a *foutah* – a piece of silk that is worn like an apron over the dress – with coloured ribbons. A wide tunic that was covered in flowers gave her a dignified appearance. She did not miss a single word that was spoken in her surrounding. She answered; then she laughed fully, rejoiced in the compliments and laughed again. Her eyes narrowed and became narrow slits in her fleshy face – then they vanished completely. She was overwhelmed with happiness. She ruled over all these women. In her, a flame was burning, erect and lucid, which seemed to dissolve the contours of her heavy body.

Omar felt she was observing him. In the same moment his aunt's soft hand had seized him by the arm and had pulled him out of the cluster of boys that surrounded him.

'Go and sit with your mother,' she whispered to him. 'She is over there.'

She pointed over to Aini with her finger. 'Go, before all the food has been eaten.'

Nimbly the boy wound his way between the guests who sat glued to the *meidas*.

'So there you are,' Aini said, when she saw him. She considered it correct to adopt a strict tone in front of the other women. 'Sit down here!'

She moved a little to the side and made room for him between herself and a strange woman. She was a small woman who swallowed morsel after morsel with bent head. She seemed completely isolated from her turbulent surroundings. Omar was watching her. With dreadful munching noises she was swallowing a piece of meat.

'One could almost think that certain women have nothing to eat at home,' a neighbour was crying. 'Bah!'

Either the other one had not heard this allusion, or else she pretended to be deaf. She did not notice the remark. Without saying a word, she continued to dig around in common dish with the thumb, index finger and middle finger. The woman who had addressed her thus had a beautiful, clean-cut face that looked superior and imposing; surely she was the wife of a merchant or carpet weaver. Aini said nothing. All the same she gave her neighbour some stealthy looks and suddenly anger was reflected in her eyes.

She turned to her son: 'Eat now!' she commanded. She broke her piece of bread and passed a part over to him; then she watched him with wrinkled brow.

The boy moved his hand towards the dish and dipped his bread into it without enthusiasm. A moment later he stopped; his throat seemed tightened, he could not eat any more.

Aini too was eating, as if she were performing a duty.

Not far away, on a neighbouring table, Aouisga and Meriem were chewing every bite with great difficulty.

'Aren't you hungry?' Aini asked her son.

The woman with the distinguished face interfered: 'This child has not eaten at all.'

'Yes, he has, little sister,' Aini excused him.

'Go and play, my child,' she said with gentle and firm voice.

The boy looked at the bread that had been left on the *meidas* with a kind of fascination. Then he went away. He could not have expressed what went on in his head. The feeling of which he became aware with intolerable clarity was a painful surprise. It filled him like burning. The question rose in him: 'Why am I deprived of this bread?' Soon followed by a second one: 'Who deprives me of this bread?' This milky white bread kneaded from white flour and these cakes which the maids were just passing around – his aunt never had to go without them.

It appeared that all the children of the town had found out about the ceremony. They appeared in large gangs. Shy, and quite black, they carefully approached the tables and sniffed. People threw them a bone or a piece of bread and drove them away with a slap. They fled to other groups.

Three of them stood there for a long time rigid and immobile; their noses in the air, they were breathing in the smells. Their feverish eyes were fixed on the guests who could not finish eating, and they followed every movement. When something was given to them, the strongest of the three seized it. The other two continued to observe the greedily eating women.

The frightening noise grew from minute to minute. Calls, shouts, screaming orders, a thousand conversations, the wailing of the tired-out cooks and the barking of dogs – all these sounds mingled in the air. This lasted only a minute. The crowd of the hungry was pushed back to the gate, which was bolted and carefully guarded by two Negro women. But in the meantime the children had undertaken a reckless raid. Pieces of meat disappeared like lightning, greedy hands seized quarter loaves of bread. Beautifully decorated plates were destroyed with a single swoop of a hand. Handfuls of raisins disappeared. . . Aunt Hasna was fussing about, as if she no longer knew what to do. And once again the vigilant Negro women at the gate were overcome in a furious attack, and the army of cripples, beggars and homeless burst open the gates that stood between them and the feasting guests. All these people were on the move; threatening, showing teeth and claws, they had surrounded the entrance and were now stampeding the wedding feast. Nobody knew what was going on. Within seconds the house was shaking with confusion. Omar was pushed roughly into a corner. Noise and confusion grew and reached their climax. The guests were bewildered and shouted madly. Meanwhile the hungry demons spread over the courtyard, the rooms, the kitchen, mounted the galleries of the first floor

and took possession of the terrace. The people of the house
rushed at them in order drive them back. There was a general
confusion. The miserable screaming of babies was heard above
all the noise.

It took a long time before order was restored.

It was a long time before calm finally returned. And now, in an
atmosphere that was breathing peace once more, a short rhythm
sounded from a little drum. The feast began. The guests rushed
around, the chatter ceased, and while the drums sounded more
festively, the women formed a circle that filled the whole
courtyard.

Singers raised their voices; one after the other everyone sang
in her own manner.

> Aicha my lady,
> Oh my darling
> Aicha my lady,
> Daughter of Bouziane. . . .

The drum beats and the songs which developed freely without
any logical sequence became monotonous after a while.

'Zohra, get up! By God, you must dance. You will show all
these women.'

It was Aunt Hasna who was calling out in a thunderous voice.
A young girl, half annoyed, half furious, received the looks that
supported this request. The women in the audience were all
beautifully decked out in wide muslin robes and fiery coloured
brocade kaftan. Precious stones were sparkling on their bosoms.
Gold-embroidered head-ties covered their hair.

'Give me the pleasure,' Aunt Hasna cried again. 'Go, little
dove . . . show them!'

Other women were also begging, and finally the dancer agreed
and got up. With lowered eyelids and pouting mouth she moved
towards the centre of the courtyard of which a large section
had been cleared. She raised her strong round arms and with
both hands she held a green silk cloth before her face. A smile
moved over her lips. The luscious young beauty moved with

a hardly visible gliding of the feet, while her arms were swaying.

But the bride was deserted. A few relatives surrounded her in the back room where she sat on her throne of honour. During the whole time, while everybody was enjoying themselves she had to remain quiet and rigid, her face covered with the impenetrable veil of the married woman.

Outside the dancer was still moving erect. Her eyes smiled faintly, her half open lips trembled. Aunt Hasna shook her head and shouted: 'What posture you have, little mother! A real princess, God is my witness!'

Now Omar did not think of anything, did not remember his condition as a hungry animal. Moved by the sight he forgot all dishes; he did not think of his pain which had become blurred and far away.

And so he was happy, he too. Somehow he was proud. Life does not only mean eating, and the happiness of life is not only the happiness of eating.

The Descendants ❀ OUSMANE SOCÉ

On the opposite bank one could see the President's palace towering above the white houses, the tall palm trees of N'Dar-Toute and the minaret of a mosque.

It was a peaceful sight, and Karim loved to survey his native town in the afternoon, when the sun was high in the sky.

Saint-Louis du Senegal, an ancient French city, had set the tone in Senegal during the nineteenth century with its elegance and its manners.

Nowadays Saint-Louis has been surpassed by young flourishing towns like Dakar. But the city has retained its oriental splendour and pompous cremonies which betray the Arabic influence.

Karim was a young man of twenty-two years. He was tall, slender and strong; his skin was brown like tobacco, and his hair chestnut coloured. His teeth gleamed like mother of pearl and adorned his smile.

Because of his perfect manners, he was accepted by the elders as a serious, diligent young man. He was good-tempered and good-humoured and always helpful. But when girls were around he was a bit of a braggart.

He had attended a French school, and after his military service, he had joined a commercial house. The adding up of long columns of figures soon tired him out. He much preferred to manipulate the huge account books. That always looked impressive, when young ladies were passing outside, smiling sweetly.

One Saturday afternoon a whole bunch of girls passed by.

They stopped, leant on the low window-sill and shouted in unison: 'Karim, Karim!'

And then followed the usual meaningless chatter of young people in love.

'Karim, haven't you any refreshments for us?' said the boldest of them.

'Had I known you were coming, I would have prepared delicious things for you.'

'Well, we'll believe you.'

'But surely, you could produce some Cola nuts,' insisted another one.

'But of course,' replied Karim, and gave them a hundred francs.

'Thank you, Karim, you are unique in the whole of Saint-Louis!'

During the whole scene, one of the young girls had stood aside. Her skin was bronze-coloured, she wore a blue muslin dress. Her hair gleamed like metal and her almond-shaped eyes were deep black.

Karim was watching her secretly, quite bewitched by her beauty. Already he was wondering how he could conquer her.

When his pretty visitors left, he moved the pencil through his hair – lost in thought. Then he got up, leant out of the window, and called Fatu, the eldest, to come back.

'What again, Karim?'

'Come a little closer, Fatu.'

She came up to the window.

'Who is that dark-haired girl in the blue muslin dress?'

'Marième,' Fatu said, smiling.

'And where does she live?'

'In the north end of the town. Next door to us.'

'Has she got a boy friend?'

'Yes, surely. But they quarrelled again on Sunday. I think they will split up.'

'All the better. Listen, Fatu, you must do me a favour. Go to

her, and tell her that I love her, and that I shall visit her tonight.
Fatu, you must help me. Tell Marième about me, and put me in
a favourable light.'

'Of course. You can rely on me. And you will surely be successful! But if I can offer some advice: be generous tonight!
Show her that you don't belong to those young men who can
hardly afford a cigarette.'

'Oh, but that's understood. I will throw money about, like
king Maissa Tenda!'

Fatu left.

Karim continued to dream. Finally he looked at the clock:

'Four o'clock! For a whole hour, I have to hang around
here.'

Automatically he put his hand in his pocket and brought out
his purse.

'Three hundred francs!'

That was all he had left of his salary. And today was only the
fifth! And what about the bill from Bertin & Co. that had come
in the morning?

Oh well, let it wait till next month. All that was unimportant
now. Right now, only Marième existed. He simply had to
conquer her, at all costs.

Karim started. Happily he counted the five strokes of the
clock. He carefully put his ledgers aside, put the fez on his head
and left for home. He lived in the southern part of town.

On his way he bought some white slippers in a Moroccan
bazaar. Happy and excited, he arrived at home. Immediately he
changed. He chose a pair of wide cotton trousers, Algerian style,
a white silk shirt and a richly embroidered bubu. Then he slipped
into his white shoes and enjoyed the reflection of his white
clothes in the blue-black henna with which he had painted his
feet.

After he had combed carefully and sprinkled himself with
heavy scent, he put the purse, cigarettes and handkerchief into
the only pocket of his trousers.

'Aren't you staying for supper?' his young sister asked him.

'No, Khagy. I am not hungry. Tell mother not to wait.'

Then he called on his best friends, Mussa, Aliune and Samba. They were to follow him to Marième.

'My brothers,' he said, 'today I must win a great victory. Today you prove that you are indeed my brothers.'

'But you know, Karim: for your sake we let ourselves be hacked in pieces; we walk through fire!'

Happily bragging they reached Marième's house. Aliune knocked.

'Come in!'

Marième sat on her couch. She wore a blouse with half-long, puffy sleeves, and her silky skin gleamed through the embroidery. Numerous gold armlets adorned her thin wrists, earrings dangled near her gently inclined neck, and a *Louis d'Or* was hanging from her black plaits on to the forehead. Her wrapper was of hand-woven Wolof material. Karim sat beside her. His friends sat in the chairs along the walls.

Karim looked around the room. There was a cupboard with mirrors and large photographs of relatives and friends hung on the walls. Little objects were placed everywhere on coloured cloths – an ostrich egg, a delicate calabash. The electric light that hung from the ceiling gave a bright light.

Silently the Senegalese men sat on their chairs. Their bubus, as white as the brightest moon and heavy with folds, gave them a majestic look.

Mussa spoke first:

'Why so silent, sister Marième?'

But the young lady was shy in the presence of so many splendidly dressed men and she was dizzy with all their perfume. She could not utter a sound. She replied with a soft smile. . .

Without knocking, young girls entered the room. They were friends of Marième, who had asked them to receive the visitors.

'What is your name, sister?' Semba asked the girl sitting beside him.

'Rokhaja.'

'Rokhaja, do you know the young men who are assembled here?'

'I don't, my brother.'

'We are Samba Lingueres.'

'That may be so. But what is a Samba Linguere?'

'A Samba Linguere is a man who in ancient times confronted any kind of enemy. The singers praised his fame for he gave away all his possessions and distributed them among the poor. He loved honour above all, and he struck down anyone who crossed him. Nowadays a Samba Linguere is a man who can face any situation and lives up to any challenge. Our friend Karim, who is wooing Marième today, is such a Samba Linguere. He is worthy to be her friend. He will prove it to you.' Then he turned to Marième herself. 'What do you say to that?'

'I am sure you are talking the truth. Everything you say sounds very convincing.'

Karim trembled with joy. Semba gave him a knowing look, which he answered with a wink.

'Call musicians!' Rokhaja said to Aliune. 'They shall entertain us.'

Senegalese singers and musicians greeted the guests.

'*Salem aleikum. Guer-Gni.*'

'*Aleikum salem.*'

They settled down on the mats that covered the floor. The guitar player tuned his instrument and began to play the song of Sundjata.

The conversation stopped. Soft tones sounded in rhythmic succession – it was the accompaniment to King Sundjata's war song – a noble, heroic and sad music, that transferred the listeners back into the times of proud African kings, to whom victory alone was the highest honour.

The singers murmured words to the music. Pensive and silent, the young people listened.

Karim put his hand in his pocket, pulled out a hundred francs note and placed it before the guitar player. The guitar player took it and thanked him:

'Oh Karim, descendant of Kuma Borso, who died a hero's death under the large tree of Salum. Oh Karim, you are among the most noble, pride of your lineage! Marième, none other can be worthy to be your lover.'

'Truly, it is so,' the singers shouted in chorus.

And now they in turn began to praise Karim, lest the guitar player alone should be rewarded. The guitar player tried to continue, but the chorus of singers drowned his soft music. Their song praised the ancestors of Karim, and reported the heroic deeds that had brought them fame and glory. The young man trembled with courage, he was determined to be a hero himself; if at this moment, enemies had appeared with lances, swords and daneguns, he would have thrust himself on them in order to conquer or die, like his ancestors whose courage was just being praised.

Karim gave the singers a hundred francs and all his friends added more money.

'Bravo, bravo,' the musicians shouted.

'These are brave heroes, Marième, accept the offer of their friendship. You will never regret it.'

'Shall we go?' Karim asked his escorts.

They agreed.

He let a little while pass, before he put on his slippers and was the last to go. Marième accompanied him to the door. When they had embraced in front of the door, the lovers said good night.

Marième returned to her girl friends, who received her laughing.

'Truly Marième, you have found a real Samba Linguere! He has given the players two hundred francs, and his friends did no less nobly.'

'He is magnificent,' said Marième.

Zebra ✿ MOULOUD MAMMERI

Because he was descended from the Prophet, the 'Zebra' had recited the Koran every evening after the French lesson. Frankly speaking, he was not very diligent. His teacher had a toothless mouth, a shrieking voice and a large stick. He was very short sighted but did not seem to bother about it. He simply assumed that God had weakened his eyesight in order to enable him the better to penetrate his soul with his inner eye. That is why the students played tricks on him, and if the Zebra went to the evening school from time to time it was mostly to enjoy this fun. Only the devil could know whether anyone had learned anything at all – though fear of his father might have helped, because the latter did not joke about these matters.

As he failed in the final examination at school, he was sent to the *Zaouia* of Sidi Mansour where he was to improve his knowledge; because he was a descendent of the Prophet and as such was expected to know at least the laws without fail.

For years he studied them fervently, by thrusting himself with great delight and with all the eagerness of his sixteen years into old manuscripts with faded letters, which had been worn out by the hands of innumerable young students. He had ardently desired to become a source of knowledge, in order to earn the esteem of men and the grace of God, for all science is futile if it does not lead to God.

In the morning, as soon as daylight fell through the cracks of his cell door, the Zebra rose from the mat on which he had slept. If it was not his turn to light the common fire he performed the ablutions with cold water, summer and winter; then, according to the rules, he addressed his first prayer to God before sunrise.

Immediately after that, the lessons began. Sheik Abdelaziz taught grammar. One had to learn the thousand verses of the textbook by heart, the verses with which Djerroum had noted down the rules with the examples. That took up the whole morning.

After that came the black soup, in which a few vegetables were swimming about, and which was cooked by the students in turn. Then they studied law and reading, which was interrupted by the prescribed five prayers. In the evening, after the last prayer, the prayer of Aisha, the Zebra returned to his cell, thirsting for knowledge; for the flood of words that had been surging around his head all day had not been able to satisfy his desire. He would have liked to know what was behind these words. But it was not permissible to interrupt the Sheik or put questions to him, as if one tried to examine him. Maybe certain types of knowledge are merely a temptation of evil. God is wisest.

One day he had met a student of the Oulemas, one of those new schools that imitate the schools of the Christians (as if anything good could ever come from the teaching of the infidels!). At first he had treated him with contempt, but then he had dared to put difficult questions to him about the doctrine, which could hardly be answered without sacrilege. The other one plainly admitted that he didn't know anything; but that did not seem to worry him very much. On the other hand he had the strange habit of translating certain Suras of the Holy Book, which is entirely useless and even dangerous, because the Koran was created in order to be learned and recited in its original form so as to enable one to quote from it emphatically on the right occasions. Of course it also contains practical rules of life, but those are widely known.

By posing complex questions to the student of the Oulemas, the Zebra finally arrived at posing questions to himself. Admittedly he was a bit reckless, and probably destined for Hell. By God, that student did not know much either, but he could explain everything the Zebra had learnt during the night while

his eyes were reddened by the smoke of the lamp. All these magic
words, whose rhythm had lulled him for years appeared to have a
meaning, sometimes a marvellous meaning. And as the sounds
ceased to be mere incantations and cradling music, it seemed to
the Zebra that the shadows fell from his eyes. Before his live
intelligence everything in the world began to fall into place with
magnificent simplicity. Everything comes from God – and everything returns to him; he had already known that; but through the
translations of the student this certainty became anchored in
consistent lines of thought and irrefutable proofs.

The climax came when he heard from the student that poets
had sung of love, of flowers and wine, of fame and war, even in
the language of the Prophet. So far he had always believed that
one could use the language of the prophet only for the revealed
truths or the categorical rules of the law. First he was hiding
himself, and was convinced that he had sold himself to the devil,
when he chanted of God and the beloved in the same words
and the same melody. Sometimes, perfidiously, the profane
language seemed even sweeter. But the student finally won him
over.

He was never quite sure whether this was not a bait of the
devil. In order to deceive him, without, however, leaving this
earth which had obtained the taste of a delightful, juicy fruit that
is melting on one's tongue, he borrowed history books from the
student. It was wonderful, what human beings had achieved!
How different and inventive they were, cruel like wolves and
good like bread! First he had gone through the centuries of
ignorance, the Dhahilia; then the Prophet had come – may the
prayers and salvation be with him – and he had brought the light
and the word of God into the world. The Zebra read the ancient
chronicles with great amazement. But to his own disapproval he
was not so much attracted by the periods of the pious conquerors,
but by the descriptions and tales of the luxuriant and flowering
times: the rich Baghdad, the radiant Andalusia, the centuries of
perfumes, odalisks and poets. He would have liked to live in the

times of Harun the Just, in order to travel from town to town, in order to collect knowledge in the entire realm.

The student of the Oulemas also gave him the history of the 'Island Maghreb' to read. Night after night he was thrilled by our past glory. Our present humiliation appeared to him even more unbearable. Certainly, it is God who lifts up and humiliates. But the Zebra learnt from the student that men all the same gave a little push to the divine will. He wrote antithetic verses about the position of the Maghreb, some gentle some excited, but always very definite. All that happened in that year.

When he returned obediently to sit on the mat beside his grammar teacher he felt the weight of an undefined heavy sorrow on his shoulders: he always felt a kind of amused respect for his teacher, but he had lost his faith. What was the use of remaining awake near the sooty lamp in order to learn empty rules, while the world was so wide and marvellous and varied that a single day spent in any place was worth as much as the entire science of the likeable, learned and insignificant teachers, that he had scraped together night after night. Outwardly he had not changed. He always wore the same radiantly white turban over his eyes, which he lowered modestly before his teachers; with customary zeal he collected oil and eggs in the villages; he missed no single prayer; he wore the circular beard, as was befitting for a Taleb; he retained his leanness, which bore witness to his diligence and his contempt for worldly matters; he fulfilled his duties when it was his turn of sweeping, fire making and cooking; and finally he kept awake as before. He kept awake, but these night hours were no longer devoted to his studies: on a yellow manuscript on whose pages the names of Allah had been entered in red, the Zebra spread out the profane pages of a pamphlet that the student had lent him. And nearly every evening, according to his inspiration he wrote verses, verses in the language of the Prophet or in his native berber language which he had learnt from his mother, when she rocked him. When one of his co-students or his teacher approached, he hid the pamphlet behind the pious manuscript, with lowered eyes he scanned aloud the texts of the truest prophetic tradition.

The verses of the Zebra were all sad or revolutionary – perhaps because those of Mohandou-Mohand, whom he loved passionately, were like that too – but in any case they were truly felt and well constructed; so well created, that the Zebra was moved to tears when he re-read these verses later by himself, in which he had sung of the past glories and the present eclipse of the 'Island of Maghreb'.

He spent another year with the laws and the verses of the Koran, collected the eggs and the oil from door to door, and felt hungrier every day. After two years he exchanged the seminar for the barracks.

He never became quite conscious of his new life. Certainly there were a few conspicuous similarities with the old life: the compulsion, the male company. But these were superficial things. No, it was certainly no longer the same thing.

When they sent him to the Mareth line in southern Tunisia to fight Rommel's troops, the desert reminded him of his verses.

After the evening soup, when all his comrades went to look for adventures – always a very specific type of adventure – the Zebra set out into the desert. While the wind swept over the dunes, he declaimed the immortal verses of the fate of the Maghreb.

Was it the wind, the atmosphere of war, the call of the dunes or that of his brethren? In any case the Zebra finally found that his fate was bitter: life seemed senseless and his actions pointless. In the seminar the fire-making, cooking and collecting had been actions that seemed to make sense with regard to the one great aim: the labour for knowledge. Here it seemed to him as if the compulsion, the drill and the training in arms had nothing to do with him, the Zebra. The problem of the broken staff arose: to continue living he had to join the ends together again. Otherwise he would have to die, he felt certain of that.

Well, one evening, after an attack on the Mareth line, instead of returning like the rest – with the exception of those, of course, who shall never return anywhere again – he walked eastwards into the desert. He had made long inquiries among the local people. When he was sure they could not catch him again, he stopped in order to take breath, and in the wind, in the night, in the sand, in this rocky place he recited the heroic poem of Antara. The world seemed to widen out to him. He breathed deeply: the air had a new taste. He thought that he would soon be in Egypt, the land of Misr, with the bewitching name, where true Muslims were still living with glowing faith, according to the law of the Prophet, and according to the divine precepts – and he forgot that he was hungry.

The road was tiresome, because God tries his chosen. The Zebra thrilled his Muslim brothers in Libya with his religious zeal and the beautiful poems he recited to them. But most of them had little enough to eat themselves and he found ample opportunity of going hungry.

At last he reached the Egyptian border. On top of his uniform he carried a somewhat strange overcoat, which he had stolen from one of the rich citizens of Tripoli, who, in contrast to the water carriers and peasants, had appreciated neither his piousness nor his poetry. For three days he remained on a military post where he was searched three or four times. 'Once they have understood that I am a Muslim,' the Zebra said to himself, 'a real Muslim as from the old days, like the fighters of the holy wars, then they will apologize, they will kiss my shoulder in the name of the Prophet, will feed me and recruit me. At last I will enter into Islam, and when I fight, I will know what I am fighting for.'

The Egyptian lieutenant, who was first worried then bored with the declarations of the Zebra, told him bluntly that he considered him a spy in French pay and that he would deliver him to the Egyptian military court, where he would have ample opportunity to prove his innocence.

The Zebra no longer knew what saints to appeal to: he was a deserter in France, a spy in Egypt and useless in Tripolitania. At

the moment, by the way, he was in prison. He could not do anything except recite poems or chant the Koran, two things which
apparently did not interest the Egyptian lieutenant very much.
After a few days he gathered that the lieutenant might be glad to
be rid of the poet, on condition that he would refrain from enter-
ing the land of the Misr. One evening the Zebra took advantage
of the deliberate negligence of a guard in order to escape. Dis-
appointed, but not angry, he proceeded westwards without
having set foot in the promised land.

He was strolling around a British camp in the hope that he
might be caught and posted in some useful situation. But only the
first happened. Once again he was imprisoned, cross-examined
and mildly beaten in order to make him confess that he was a spy
in German pay. That was certainly a provocation. He confessed
nothing. In order to get out of the affair he finally produced the
following argument which he considered to be irrefutable: 'Do
you really think that if the Germans needed a spy they would
pick on a Zebra like myself?' From this day onwards he became
the Zebra for everybody.[1]

The British commander was finally convinced of the truth of
this statement and he returned him to Tunisia where he handed
him over to the French authorities. For months the Zebra
recited poems in a prison, which made him think nostalgically of
the hunger and the thirst he had experienced in the desert. But
since one needed men, and since one was finally convinced that
he was nothing but a small comical Zebra he was eventually
shipped over to France.

He found the country of the infidels very beautiful. He
would have liked to remain there, but the Germans (whom,
incidentally, he never saw) drove him right down to Marseilles.
Reluctantly he returned to his sun, which he considered to be
hostile.

But happily he began to realize that he was not the only one
who desired new life for the Maghreb. Others had had the same

[1] *Zèbre* or *drôle de Zèbre* is colloquial for 'poor devil' or 'queer fellow'.

idea: of course, they did not write poetry, but they had formed parties. The Zebra joined the ones that seemed to come closest to his own wishes.

Yet it was an accident that one morning, when he was slouching along on the worn-out soles of his sandals through the Rue Colonna d'Orlano he met groups of young men, also in sandals, whose countenance was disturbed, furious or enthusiastic. He asked one of them where they were going, all so frightened and wild. But the man abused him. Another one told him that fifty-six national resistance fighters were being condemned by the law court: 'Martyrs, my brother!' The Zebra could not understand everything because of the noise. Some cried 'Murderers!', but the Zebra did not know who was meant. Others wanted the political prisoners to be freed. The Zebra felt his lungs widening, as on the day on which he had fled into the dunes. He sensed in himself the heroic soul of the Almohadic warriors, who led their horses from Cordoba to Gabes, and he followed the most excited group.

He mounted and reached the Rue Dumont d'Urville. A group of screaming young men carried him along and threw him down. He had lost his sandals. From all sides people were trampling on him. He was still lying on the ground, when two heavy boots appeared before his eyes. He lifted his head and saw a policeman who hid the sun from him. A kick made him jump up. He received indiscriminate punches, was pushed from hand to hand and was finally shoved into a carriage that was dark inside.

After six months he was freed, and for a month he drifted about in the towns and villages and farms, sleeping on benches, in porticos and on God's earth. He tried to get back into prison, where at least he would have found food and a roof over his head. He did not succeed. He stole reluctantly and started a fight with another unemployed, only a few steps away from a policeman, who deliberately ignored him.

One day, he hardly knew how, he found himself before the

pointed arch of the gate, where once, during countless days and nights, he had chanted the verses of the Holy Book. He pushed the door open. A very young taleb struggled with the fire. 'Go to sleep, brother, let me do it. I am used to it,' the Zebra told him. Then he kissed the head of the Sheik, who received him, as if he had left but yesterday. He spoke the morning prayer, together with all the other talebs. He had forgotten nothing, neither the words nor the gestures; but his knees pained him, because he was no longer used to bending his legs.

He squatted on the old mat, and listened to the modulating, crystal clear, almost transcendental voice of his teacher, who commented on the law and the word of God. He practised all the verses, took his turn in the menial jobs and tried to rediscover the zeal of former days. After ten weeks it was his turn again to light the fire, just after the small beardless taleb. It was this very same taleb who found the Zebra stretched out near the brazier in which the fire burned. He had drawn the hood of his burnous over his face. The little taleb touched him with his foot and pulled the hood back: the eyes of the Zebra were opened and glazed. He had stopped suffering.

Before his death the Zebra had written a letter in which he took leave of his teacher and all the talebs. The close of the letter in particular caused displeasure: 'I forgive you all the evil I have done unto you, because I might have done it to others . . . I can no longer live for nothing, as you all are doing; I can no longer do it . . . but I have tried it for a long time, with all my soul, that is to say, if I had one. I swear this by God'.

A furious taleb cried that all this was just one big blasphemy; the letter ought to be burnt and the corpse ought to be thrown to the dogs. Not all shared this view. The teacher was asked for his opinion. The teacher shut his bloodless lips with his bony index finger. Silence alone is befitting in the presence of death, which cannot be reached by our anger or our love. God alone can judge the souls he has created.

On the same evening they buried the Zebra next to the tomb of the Saint of the Zaouia, although he was the pupil who had deserved this least. He had died, because he did not know what to do with his ineradicable love for the 'Island Maghreb' and because he had wished, like the infidels, that his life should serve some purpose.

Ambiguous ❀ SHEIKH AMIDOU
Adventure   KANE

An Extract from L'Aventure Ambiguë

TRANSLATED BY
WENDY SPIEGEL

When the madman came, he found the master in the same position lying down, one arm along his body, the other over his eyes.

The man was wrapped in an old frock coat. His slightest gesture revealed that he wore the full habit of the Diallobe. The frock coat's age, its questionable cleanliness compared to the immaculate *boubous* gave him an unusual quality. His appearance, like his clothes, also left a strange impression. His features were motionless with the exception of his eyes where there was a continual restlessness. One might have said that he knew an uncanny secret harmful to the world which he constantly strove not to reveal. He had a shifting glance. Expressions were destroyed almost as soon as they were born. One doubted that he could have a single lucid thought.

He had spoken very little since they had named him 'the madman'.

This man, who was an authentic son of the region, had once gone away. Even his family had not known where he went. He had remained away for many years. Then one morning he came back, dressed in his frock coat. When he returned he talked all the time. He claimed that he had come back from the whiteman's country and that there he had fought against the whites. In the beginning one took him at his word, although none of the other sons of the region, who had been in the war against the whites, reported having seen him there. But soon one began to question what he said.

At first his tale was so extravagant that it was difficult to

believe him. But even more than this extravagance, it was the
mimicry of the man which was alarming. For while he spoke the
madman began to relive, as if delirious, the circumstances of his
tale. One day, explaining how he had been wounded in the
stomach – he did, in fact, have a scar there – the man suddenly
shrivelled up, then fell down, his arms to his stomach gasping in
agony. A long fever had followed. Since then they contrived to
avoid him, while he himself only recovered from his fits in order
to search for obliging listeners. Before them, he dramatically
relived his memories.

One day, he learned that he had been named 'the madman'.
Then he was silent. Nevertheless the name remained.

The man sat down next to the master whom he believed asleep
and waited for him to awaken.

'Ah! Is it you? What are you doing here?'

'They wear you out a lot, all those people, don't they?'

And the madman vaguely designated the houses around the
master's home.

'Chase them away. You will chase them away, won't you, the
next time they come?'

His glittering look seemed, for a fraction of a second, to be
anxiously awaiting an answer.

'Tell me you'll chase them away . . .'

'Yes, I will.'

The man became calm.

'Now they come to you. They are as humble and sweet as
lambs. But don't let that fool you. At heart, they are not lambs.
It's because you are still here, with your empty house and your
old clothes, that they are still lambs. But you are going to die.
Then they will change, I assure you; as soon as you die. You
alone delay their metamorphosis.'

He leaned over and passionately kissed the master's hand. The
master started and pulled back his hand as if it had been burned.
Then, reconsidering, he gave it back to the madman who began
to stroke it.

'You see, when you die, all these straw huts will die with you. Everything here will be as it is there. You know, there . . .'

The master, who was still lying down, wanted to get up, but the madman gently held him back. He drew a little nearer and carefully raising the master's head, he placed it comfortably on his lap.

'What's is it like there?' asked the master.

A furtive expression of joy flashed across the madman's face.

'Really? Do you want me to tell you?'

'Yes, tell me.'

And then the madman spoke:

'It was the morning that I landed there. From the very beginning I felt an unspeakable anguish. It seemed that my heart and my body were shrivelling up. I shuddered and went back to the huge landing shed. My legs were limp and trembling. I wanted desperately to sit down. Around me the tile-floor was like a glittering mirror which echoed the sound of footsteps. In the middle of the immense shed I noticed several armchairs. But I had hardly looked over there when once again I felt myself shrivelling. It was as if my whole body was rebelling. I put down my suitcases and sat on the cold tiling. Around me, the passers-by stopped. A woman came over to me. She spoke to me. I thought she was asking if I felt well. My body became quiet despite the cold of the tiling which penetrated my bones. I lowered my hands on the icy floor. I even had the desire to take off my shoes, in order to touch the glittering sea-green mirror. But I was vaguely aware of an incongruity. I simply extended my legs on the chilling block.'

The master raised himself a little to meet the look of the madman. He was struck by the sudden coherence of the tale. His amazement grew when he saw that this look was fixed. He had never seen him like this. The master put his head back on the madman's lap. He realized that the man was trembling slightly.

'Already a small group had gathered around me. A man pushed his way to me and took me by the wrist. Then he beckoned to

someone to put me on a nearby sofa. Eager hands were held out
to lift me up. I kept them off and stood up by myself, rising above
the group. I had recovered my serenity and now that I was
standing, there was nothing about me that did not appear stable
and sane. Around me, I sensed the people consulting, surprised
at my sudden recovery. I sputtered out words of excuse. Then,
bending down, I took a heavy suitcase in each hand and went
through the circle of wondering spectators. But I was hardly in
the street when once again I felt myself shrivelling. I concealed it
with considerable effort and hurried away from there. Behind
me, I sensed everyone staring from the immense room. I turned a
corner and finding an entrance-way sheltered from the passers-by,
I sat down on one of my suitcases. It was just in time for my
trembling had once again become apparent. What I felt was more
than my body's rebellion. Now that I was sitting down, the
trembling again diminished. It had seemed to correspond to my
inner anguish. A man, passing by, wanted to stop. I turned my
head. He hesitated, then, shaking his head, continued on his way.
I watched him go. His back was lost among other backs, his grey
suit among other grey suits. The hard sound of his shoes mingled
with the sound of others which rang out on the asphalt. The
asphalt . . . I glanced over the whole expanse and saw no end to
the stone. There the ice of the felspar, here the clear grey of the
stone, this lustreless black of asphalt. Nowhere the fresh softness
of the bare earth. Over the hard asphalt, my eyes thirsted in vain
for an unadorned foot. But there were no feet. On the hard stone,
nothing but the cracking of a thousand egg-shells. Had man no
longer feet of flesh? A woman went by. Her pink calves hardened
weirdly into two black spikes. Since I had arrived I hadn't seen a
single foot. All I saw was the tide of shells sweeping over the
asphalt. Everywhere, from the ground to the top of the buildings,
the bare and resonant shell made the street into a granite basin.
This valley of stone was split by a fantastic river of maddened
machines. I was familiar with automobiles. Yet never had they
seemed so sovereign and desperate. On the street where they

had precedence, not one human being walked. I had never seen that, master of the Diallobe. There, before me, in the midst of that great mass of inhabited dwellings, I contemplated an inhuman vista, devoid of men. Imagine, master, in the very heart of what man has made, an expanse forbidden to his own flesh, even to his bare feet. . . .'

'Is that really true? Can it be true that in the heart of his own dwelling the furtive silhouette of man only knows confined spaces?'

The madman trembled with joy, seeing how well he had been understood.

'Yes, I saw him. You know, master, the fragile silhouette which leans upon one leg, then the other, in order to advance . . .'

'Well?'

'I have seen him, in his own dwelling of confined spaces. Machines reigned there.'

The madman was silent. For a long time the two men didn't speak; then, gently, the master asked:

'What else did you see?'

'Really? Do you want me to tell you?'

'Yes, tell me.'

'I saw the machines. They are shells, twisted into many forms, and move as they will. But, you know that the expanse has no inner life at all; it has, therefore, nothing to lose. It cannot be hurt, like the silhouette, but only become further twisted. Also, it has driven back the silhouette, easily frightened, and has destroyed its inner life.'

'I understand, go on.'

'This expanse is autonomous. But, you know that it is the stability itself which makes the movement apparent. And now it has begun to move. Its movement is more complete than the jerky advance of the hesitant silhouette. It cannot fall, where would it fall? Also, it has driven back the silhouette, easily frightened, and destroyed its movement.'

The madman was silent. The master, supporting himself on

his elbow, raised himself up and saw that the madman was weeping.

The master sat down then and drew the madman to him. The madman leaned on him, his head resting on the master's shoulder. The master wiped away his tears, then, tenderly, began to rock him.

'Master, I want to pray with you, to drive back the horde. Once more, obscene chaos is in the world and threatens us.'

❁ The Modern World

Revenge ❁ HENRI KREA

The parade ground gleams like an airfield. Crickets are heard under every blade of grass. One feels removed here from all human presence. And yet the town is barely a mile away and the river is nearby. It carries no water. In winter a torrent cascades and thunders through a long ditch in the riverbed of white and blue pebbles. The mountains are washed out, and their fiery red slopes descend steeply like huge cliffs. If one ascended the river – we certainly shan't, because the sun is burning hot now – one could see the huts of the gipsies higher up. They consist of ancient chassis of pre-war cars. Everything there is rusty. They say the gipsies eat chicken and capons and that they wring their necks. They often steal fowl that stray from the villas on to the street to feed under the cool, moist plantains. Higher up still, near the French brothel, are the tin-towns. They consist of kerosene tins and old boxes that still carry the factory labels. Sometimes neither rain nor weather succeeds in removing the paper, which sticks as if to hide all the misery under its label. *Le Chat, Marseilles Soap, Refinery of Berre.* Water trickles along the path towards the tin huts. Women walk across it, their palm leaf baskets on their heads and jars with fresh water in their hands. Children boast: 'I could have been among them, if mother hadn't married my father; he is a marvellous fellow, he always manages to get money from somewhere or other when it finishes. He is kind too. He knows everybody. Hermits and robbers. But now he is gone. They say he is in France. But I say he is in the mountains.' 'Why?' 'He is in the mountains because he joined the Maquis.' 'Why?' Hamed is always curious. 'Why? Because sometimes he comes home during the day. Last time he was dressed up as a woman. He wore a black striped haik, which the teacher's wife lent him – he is in the mountains too. They are as bold as lions.' 'I love you, freedom, I love you.' 'I always sing that.' 'He comes home during the day? Then he is not afraid.'

Of course he is not afraid. It would be awful for me, if he was afraid. Hamed admires me because my father is in the mountains. He is unhappy because he can't really say that. His father is in prison, and nobody knows how he is.

'Don't eat these peppers.'

'Why shouldn't I eat them?'

'It is not good for you. Mama always says that.'

'We have nothing else to eat at home. I stole them on the Arab market. Did you see what they have done with the Arab market?'

'Yes, I know, they have been profiting.'

'They have been profiting as long as I have known them.'

'But I love freedom! I love to sing.'

'They have shifted the market to make room for their houses. They have sent the poor into the heat, to the upper boulevard. It is out of the way too, and nobody goes there.'

'I know, I know. The vegetables spoil quickly there, because they have no water to spray them with. They are all thieves.'

'Shall I give you a riddle?'

'Yes, do.'

'What is a highway robber?'

'?'

'Do you give up?'

'I give up.'

'Think.'

'Tell me.'

'Lala, la, la, la . . .'

'Why don't you tell me? You are always singing.'

'There flies a cricket. It looks pretty, like a little fan with a rainbow over it, when the rain has stopped.'

'Tell me, tell me.'

'Who has lost? You . . . What will you give me, if I tell you?'

'But you know I haven't got anything.'

'Well?'

'Tell me at last.'

'A highway robber. . . .'

He whispered.

'. . . is a policeman.'

They burst into laughter. Kader was rolling in the grass. 'A policeman. A policeman.' A train passed in the distance. A goods train, with smoke and an old yellow locomotive. The wagons were not loaded. The train whistled. Hamed tried to imitate the hissing of the steam. Then he started to pick flowers. Kader tried to count the wagons, but there were too many. He looked at Hamed.

'Why are you picking daisies?'

'For your bride. I know everything.'

'Who is my bride?'

'I know, it is Saphia.'

'No, she is not my bride, she is yours.'

'Wait a moment. Let us see. How old are you?'

'Eleven. And you?'

'Thirteen.'

'So you are the bridegroom. I'll give you the flowers. She is ill, and her father has no money for the doctor. He asked my father, but my father said he can't give anything now, they need money in the Maquis.'

'The Mozarabs could give them something. They have enough. . . .'

'Maybe they will give them something in the end. Nobody goes to them.'

'But Saphia is ill.'

They sat thoughtfully on the slope. The crickets were chirping again. They had stopped fiddling with their wings, because of the noise from their jumping and shouting. They were quiet. Kader took a blade of grass and chewed it. Hamed tried to whistle a tune: 'I love you, Freedom, I love you,' and he stretched out in the grass. The rising wind moved the grass, even though it was short. Kader looked over the smooth extent of the parade ground. It resembles a football field. That's because it is winter. Now he stretches out too, and the sky above him is large and blue. They say that all this is beautiful, but why is it beautiful? From time to time they hear a humming noise.

'That's from the airport.'

'No, that's a helicopter.'

Kader sits up and tries to discover the machine above the plain. It is behind the mountain.

'I can't see it.'

'Maybe it collects freedom fighters.'

The previous week a helicopter had crashed over the glacier. It was shot down with a rifle. Like Zorro, the man with the whip. For a while they heard the humming of the propeller, then all was silent. The wind blew in the plantains by the roadside and a train whistled in the distance. Then Kader gets up. He has found an old tin, dribbles and shoots at imaginary goals.

'Go on. Ben Barek.'

'I am Kopa.'

'And I am Ben Barek.' And he adds proudly: 'The black pearl.'

'Wait, now I shall delude you. The black pearl. . . .' Kader has taken the tin and has run away. Hamed follows and threatens him. He trips him and Kader falls down flat. He lies motionless. Hamed has stopped laughing, but Kader has got up laughing. He looks at his legs which are green with crushed grass. He has a scratch below the knee. One sees the red flesh, as in a butcher's shop. It does not hurt, but it bleeds. Hamed tears his shirt immediately and makes a bandage. Kader looks at the blood in surprise. Is that *my* blood? *My* blood? Hamed's legs are full of scars. He is used to it. They sit down again. Hamed shows his right calf. There he has a large scar, that shines like glossy paper.

'What is that?' asks Kader.

'My uncle did that, when I was small. I did not want to go shopping. Then he got furious and threw a shovel of glowing coals at my feet. I was lucky, he only hit the calf. But when my father came home, and my mother told him about it, he beat him up terribly! Since then he is gone. He was mad.'

'The dirty pig. Where is he now?'

'I suppose he is dead.'

'Ha! That serves him right.'

'One should not wish evil to the dead. They are dead.'

'That is true.'

Kader had got up. He was limping a bit, and the leg was stiff. He had felt a bit sick, when he saw the blood. It was so strange. All *that* was in him. Up till then he had never noticed that he had a body. All *that* was of no consequence. But such a wound is terrible. Inside I am like that.

Hamed had stretched out again. He was chewing a blade of grass again and was singing: 'Freedom, I love you.'

'Hamed! Hamed! Hamed!'

Kader's voice had changed with fear. Now he opened his mouth without uttering a sound, and was beckoning desperately. Hamed ran to him immediately. His naked feet were slipping on the wet grass. He nearly stepped on an enormous blue thistle.

'Look,' said Kader.

'What's the matter?'

'There.'

'Where?'

'In the ditch.'

At first Hamed couldn't see anything. Then he distinguished a large shrunken mass, like an enormous grey ball at the bottom of the ditch.

'What's that?'

'It is a soldier. A Frenchman.'

'Poor fellow.'

'It is not his fault. Those who have money force him to wage war.'

Kader wept, and soon began to sob. Hamed remained cool.

'Do not weep. One must not weep. This could happen to your

own father. My father was beaten up, and one day he will be lying there just like that.' Kader stopped weeping. His leg was now burning. He loosened the bandage and tightened it again. The grasshoppers were chirping on the parade ground, and now and then the crickets were fiddling in the plantains and the thin shrubs. Hamed was thinking. He was thinking of the fellow who had betrayed his father. He was an acquaintance, who was always armed. For a long time he was thinking of home and hunger.

'Something must be done.'

'Something must be done.'

'We could take the weapons and bring them to the freedom fighters.'

'What shall we put them in?'

'Into the cart.'

The cart with ball bearings stood at the edge of the slope.

'Yes, we'll put everything inside and when we meet somebody I'll sit on top of the weapons and you push me.'

'Yes, yes, you have good ideas.'

They entered the ditch and took the revolver, the sten-gun, ammunition and grenades.

'And the clothes?'

'They can get those themselves. We are children.'

They load everything into the cart, which is fortunately fairly large. Suddenly Kader has a different idea.

'Shouldn't we bury them?'

'What?'

'The weapons. A little further away under the cypress trees near the brick factory.'

'Why shouldn't we carry them into the mountains?'

'Not during the day. It's too dangerous. The cart is too full.'

'Then we'll take only two or three, and hide the rest.'

The cypresses stood like a black prison wall, a gloomy fence. The cypress is the tree of the dead. It prefers to grow no cemeteries. Soon they had reached the foot of the heavy stems, the alleged masts of ancient sailing boats. The earth was as rich as clay.

The sun was quite small. He gleamed like a tiny pearl in the large white sky. On the right the mountains were glimmering. They stretched far along the sea. With pounding hearts they trudged along under the rustling trees. The cart was rolling fast over the tiny roads with their softened tarmac. When it is hot the footprints appear on the road, as in mud during the rainy season. Often they had gone to the hill to fight, to the ancient Turkish fort that dominated the town. From there one could see the entire plain with the hideous tower of St Charles's Church, from which dark bells rang continuously, as if they wanted to remind one all the time of the presence of the suppressors. Hamed told Kader that they were approaching the town.

'You must sit on the weapons, so they don't catch us.'

'Not yet.'

'At the next milestone you will sit in the cart.'

'We will alternate.'

'That's not necessary.'

'Yes, it is.'

'We will only attract attention.'

'Then I'll pull you.'

'No.'

'Why not?'

'I have a plan.'

'What is it?'

'It's a secret.'

'But we have no secrets from one another.'

'Yes; I can't tell you.'

'Please, tell me.'

'I can't. It is important.'

'You must tell me.'

'It's not necessary.'

'I am older than you.'

'You are not much older. And I can't tell you.'

'You are not a good comrade.'

So they continued silently. The wind had started blowing, and the plantains were rustling. Kader and Hamed pulled the cart, each with one arm. There was a signboard saying: 'Blida 1 km.'

'We have arrived.'

'Why?'

'Sit on the weapons.'

Kader sat on the equipment of the dead Frenchman. It was hard. He put the shoulder belt into place that was dragging on the road. Hamed pulled the cart with difficulty. He leant forward and the muscles on his lean legs were standing out. After two hundred yards he stopped and took breath.

'Swop with me now.'

'No.'

'Why?'

'I have my plan.'

In spite of Hamed's refusal, Kader got up and stretched his legs on the road. Hamed gave in and climbed on the cart; he looked like one succumbing to an adverse fate.

'It's better like this.'

'I had my plan.'

'We can swop again.'

They came to the Shell station. There was a monster on the advertising posters. There was a strong smell of petrol; Kader liked that. It seemed to be late. The people were rushing home. A dozen times they passed groups of policemen or soldiers, who paid no attention to them. They took one of the outer boulevards in order to reach the centre of the city; from the actual 'Boulevard', the street of the Europeans, they would have been driven with much fuss. They passed between the barracks of rifles and the artillery. The evening's drum roll sounded like a dark warning; the announcement of coming events. Thus the inevitability of future deeds was invented by man himself. Kader felt that with extreme consternation. He tried to think of many beautiful things, but when he looked at his and Hamed's rags he was also reminded that in spite of the slice of *pâté* in the morning he hadn't eaten 'for years'.

Night gave a flaming signal of its arrival. At the end of the plain, above the sea which Hamed had never seen, the sun sank gently behind the red hills of Sahel. They stopped still a moment in order to watch him sink into nothing – as if for the last time. The image of his purple glory remained alive in their memory. Then they were on the large square of the city. Kader heard Hamed say, 'Look at the tall one there, he has betrayed my father.' Then Hamed took the revolver, which he had probably been holding for a long time in his right hand over his heart, and he jumped out of the cart. He posted himself two yards in front of the blinded shadow and he shot and shot. The other fell without a word. Then many people came. The sun sank in all its glory behind the hills that were now black. Kader ran away, covered by the crowd, and swore to himself to avenge his comrade. Hamed had a strangely soft feeling in his legs and finally fell asleep.

The Hands of the Blacks ❁ LUIS BERNADO HONWANA

TRANSLATED BY
DOROTHY GUEDES

I don't remember now how we got on to the subject, but one day Teacher said that the palms of the black's hands were much lighter than the rest of their bodies because only a few centuries ago they walked around on all fours. like wild animals, so their palms weren't exposed to the sun, which made the rest of their bodies darker and darker. I thought of this when Father Christiano told us after catechism that we were absolutely hopeless, and that even the blacks were better than us, and he went back to this thing about their hands being lighter, and said it was like that because they always went about with their hands folded together, praying in secret. I thought this was so funny, this thing of the black's hands being lighter, that you should just see me now – I don't let go of anyone, whoever they are, until they tell me why they think that the palms of the black's hands are lighter. Dona Dores, for instance, told me that God made their hands lighter like that so they wouldn't dirty the food they made for their masters, or anything else they were ordered to do that had to be kept quite clean.

Senhor Antunes, the Coca Cola man, who only comes to the village now and again when all the Cokes in the cantinas have been sold, said to me that everything I had been told was a lot of baloney. Of course I don't know if it was really, but he assured me it was. After I said yes, all right, it was baloney, then he told me what he knew about this thing of the black's hands. It was like this: 'Long ago, many years ago, God, Our Lord Jesus Christ, the Virgin Mary, St Peter, many other saints, all the angels that were in Heaven then, and some of the people who had died and gone to Heaven – they all had a meeting and decided to make blacks. Do you know how? They got hold of some clay and pressed it into some second-hand moulds. And to bake the clay of the creatures they took them to the Heavenly kilns. Because they were in a hurry and there was no room next to the fire, they hung them in the chimneys. Smoke, smoke, smoke – and there you have them, black as coals. And now do you want to know why their hands stayed white? Well, didn't they have to hold on while their clay baked?'

When he had told me this Senhor Antunes and the other men who were around us were very pleased and they all burst out laughing. That very same day Senhor Frias called me after Senhor Antunes had gone away, and told me that everything I had heard from them there had been just one big pack of lies. Really and truly, what he knew about the black's hands was right – that God finished making men and told them to bathe in a lake in Heaven. After bathing the people were nice and white. The blacks, well, they were made very early in the morning, and at this hour the water in the lake was very cold, so they only wet the palms of their hands and the soles of their feet before dressing and coming into the world.

But I read in a book that happened to mention it, that the blacks have hands lighter like this because they spent their lives bent over, gathering the white cotton of Virginia and I don't know where else. Of course Dona Estefánia didn't agree when I told her this. According to her its only because their hands became bleached with all that washing.

Well, I don't know what to think about all this, but the truth is that however calloused and cracked they may be, a black's hands are always lighter than all the rest of him. And that's that!

My mother is the only one who must be right about this question of a black's hands being lighter than the rest of his body. On the day that we were talking about it, us two, I was telling her what I already knew about the question, and she just couldn't stop laughing. What I thought was strange was that she didn't tell me at once what she thought about all this, and she only answered me when she was sure that I wouldn't get tired of bothering her about it. And even then she was crying and clutching herself around the stomach like someone who had laughed so much that it was quite unbearable. What she said was more or less this:

'God made blacks because they had to be. They had to be, my son. He thought they really had to be. . . . Afterwards he regretted having made them because the other men laughed at them and took them off to their homes and put them to serve like slaves or not much better. But because he couldn't make them all be white, for those who were used to seeing them black would complain, He made it so that the palms of their hands would be exactly like the palms of the hands of other men. And do you know why that was? Of course you don't know, and it's not surprising, because many, many people don't know. Well, listen: it was to show that what men do is only the work of men. . . . That what men do is done by hands that are the same – hands of people who, if they had any sense, would know that before everything else they are men. He must have been thinking of this when He made the hands of the blacks be the same as the hands of those men who thank God they are not black!'

After telling me all this, my mother kissed my hands. As I ran off into the yard to play ball, I thought that I had never seen a person cry so much when nobody had hit them.

Blankets ❁ ALEX LA GUMA

Choker lay on the floor of the lean-to in the back yard where they had carried him. It was cooler under the sagging roof, with the pile of assorted junk in one corner; an ancient motor tyre, sundry split and warped boxes, an old enamel display sign with patches like maps of continents on another planet where the enamelling had cracked away, and the dusty footboard of a bed. There was also the smell of dust and chicken droppings and urine in the lean-to.

From outside, beyond a chrome-yellow rhomboid of sun, came a clatter of voices. In the yard they were discussing him. Choker opened his eyes, and peering down the length of his body, past the bare, grimy toes, he saw several pairs of legs, male and female, in tattered trousers and laddered stockings.

Somebody, a man, was saying: '. . . that was coward . . . from behind, *mos.*'

'*Ja*. But look what he done to others . . .'

Choker thought, to hell with those baskets. To hell with them all.

Somebody had thrown an old blanket over him. It smelled of sweat and having-been-slept-in-unwashed, and it was torn and threadbare and stained. He touched the exhausted blanket with thick, grubby fingers. The texture was rough in parts and shiny thin where it had worn away. He was used to blankets like this.

Choker had been stabbed three times, each time from behind. Once in the head, then between the shoulder blades and again in the right side, out in the street, by an old enemy who had once sworn to get him.

The bleeding had stopped and there was not much pain. He

had been knifed before, admittedly not as bad as this, but he thought through the pain, the basket couldn't even do a decent job. He lay there and waited for the ambulance. There was blood drying slowly on the side of his hammered-copper face, and he also had a bad headache.

The voices, now and then raised in laughter, crackled outside. Feet moved on the rough floor of the yard and a face not unlike that of a brown dog wearing an expiring cloth cap, looked in.

'You still awright, Choker? Am'ulance is coming just now, hey.'

'. . . off,' Choker said. His voice croaked.

The face withdrew, laughing: '*Ou* Choker. *Ou* Choker.'

He was feeling tired now. The grubby fingers, like corroded iron clamps, strayed over the parched field of the blanket . . . He was being taken down a wet, tarred yard with tough wire netting over the windows which looked into it. The place smelled of carbolic disinfectant, and the bunch of heavy keys clink-clinked as it swung from the hooked finger of the guard.

They reached a room fitted with shelving that was stacked here and there with piled blankets. 'Take two, *jong*,' the guard said, and Choker began to rummage through the piles, searching for the thickest and warmest blankets. But the guard, who somehow had a doggish face and wore a disintegrating cloth cap, laughed and jerked him aside, and seizing the nearest blankets, found two and flung them at Choker. They were filthy and smelly and within their folds vermin waited like irregular troops in ambush.

'Come on. Come on. You think I got time to waste?'

'It's cold, *mos*, man,' Choker said. But it wasn't the guard to whom he was talking. He was six years old and his brother, Willie, a year his senior, twisted and turned in the narrow, cramped, sagging bedstead which they shared, dragging the thin cotton blanket from Choker's body. Outside the rain slapped against the cardboard-patched window, and the wind wheezed through cracks and corners like an asthmatic old man.

'No, man, Willie, man. You got all the blanket, *jong*.'

'Well, I can't *mos* help it, man. It's cold.'

'What about me?' Choker whined. 'What about me. I'm also cold *mos*.'

Huddled together under the blanket, fitted against each other like two pieces of a jigsaw puzzle. The woman's wiry hair got into his mouth and smelled of stale brilliantine. There were dark stains made by heads, on the crumpled, grey-white pillow, and a rubbed smear of lipstick, like a half-healed wound.

The woman was saying, half-asleep, 'No, man. No, man.' Her body was wet and sweaty under the blanket, and the bed smelled of a mixture of cheap perfume, spilled powder, human bodies and infant urine. The faded curtain over the room window beckoned to him in the hot breeze. In the early slum-coloured light a torn under-garment hanging from a brass knob was a spectre in the room.

The woman turned from him under the blankets, protesting, and Choker sat up. The agonized sounds of the bedspring woke the baby in the bathtub on the floor, and it began to cry, its toothless voice rising in a high-pitched wail that grew louder and louder.

Choker opened his eyes as the wail grew to a crescendo and then quickly faded as the siren was switched off. Voices still splattered the sunlight in the yard, now excited. Choker saw the skirts of white coats and then the ambulance men were in the lean-to. His head was aching badly, and his wounds were throbbing. His face perspired like a squeezed-out wash-rag. Hands searched him. One of the ambulance attendants asked: 'Do you feel any pain?'

Choker looked at the pink-white face above him, scowling. 'No, sir.'

The layer of old newspapers on which he was lying was soaked with his blood. 'Knife wounds,' one of the attendants said. 'He isn't bleeding much,' the other said. 'Put on a couple of pressure pads.'

He was in mid-air, carried on a stretcher and flanked by a procession of onlookers. Rubber sheeting was cool against his back. The stretcher rumbled into the ambulance and the doors slammed shut, sealing off the spectators. Then the siren whined and rose, clearing a path through the crowd.

Choker felt the vibration of the ambulance through his body as it sped on its way. His murderous fingers touched the folded edge of the bedding. The sheet around him was white as cocaine, and the blanket was thick and new and warm. He lay still, listening to the siren.

The Voter ❀ CHINUA ACHEBE

Rufus Okeke – Roof, for short – was a very popular man in his village. Although the villagers did not explain it in so many words Roof's popularity was a measure of their gratitude to an energetic young man who, unlike most of his fellows nowadays, had not abandoned the village in order to seek work, any work, in the towns. And Roof was not a village lout either. Everyone knew how he had spent two years as a bicycle repairer's apprentice in Port Harcourt and had given up of his own free will a bright future to return to his people and guide them in these political times. Not that Umuofia needed a lot of guidance. The village already belong *en masse* to the People's Alliance Party, and its most illustrious son, Chief the Honourable Marcus Ibe was Minister of Culture in the outgoing government (which was pretty certain to be the incoming one as well). Nobody doubted that the Honourable Minister would be elected in his constituency. Opposition to him was like the proverbial fly trying to move a dunghill. It would have been ridiculous enough without coming, as it did now, from a complete nonentity.

As was to be expected Roof was in the service of the Honourable Minister for the coming elections. He had become a real expert in election campaigning at all levels – village, local government or national. He could tell the mood and temper of the electorate at any given time. For instance he had warned the Minister months ago about the radical change that had come into the thinking of Umuofia since the last national election.

The villagers had had five years in which to see how quickly and plentifully politics brought wealth, chieftaincy titles, doctorate degrees and other honours some of which, like the last, had still to be explained satisfactorily to them; for they still expected a doctor to heal the sick. Anyhow, these honours had come so readily to the man to whom they had given their votes free of charge five years ago that they were now ready to think again.

Their point was that only the other day Marcus Ibe was a not too successful mission school teacher. Then politics had come to their village and he had wisely joined up, some say just in time to avoid imminent dismissal arising from a female teacher's pregnancy. Today he was Chief the Honourable; he had two long cars and had just built himself the biggest house anyone had seen in those parts. But let it be said that none of these successes had gone to Marcus's head as they might have done. He remained a man of the people. Whenever he could he left the good things of the capital and returned to his village which had neither running water nor electricity. He knew the source of his good fortune, unlike the little bird who ate and drank and went out to challenge his personal spirit. Marcus had christened his new house 'Umuofia Mansions' in honour of his village and had slaughtered five bulls and countless goats to entertain the people on the day it was opened by the Archbishop.

Every one was full of praise for him. One old man said: 'Our son is a good man; he is not like the mortar which as soon as food comes its way turns its back on the ground.' But when the feasting was over the villagers told themselves that they had under-rated the power of the ballot paper before and should not do so again. Chief the Honourable Marcus Ibe was not unprepared. He had drawn five months' salary in advance, changed a few hundred pounds into shining shillings and armed his campaign boys with eloquent little jute bags. In the day he made his speeches; at night his stalwarts conducted their whispering campaign. Roof was the most trusted of these campaigners.

'We have a Minister from our village, one of our own sons,' he said to a group of elders in the house of Ogbuefi Ezenwa, a man of high traditional title. 'What greater honour can a villager have? Do you ever stop to ask yourselves why we should be singled out for this honour? I will tell you: it is because we are favoured by the leaders of P A P. Whether we cast our paper for Marcus or not P A P will continue to rule. Think of the pipe-borne water they have promised us. . . .'

Besides Roof and his assistant there were five elders in the room. An old hurricane lamp with a cracked, sooty, glass chimney gave out yellowish light in their midst. The elders sat on very low stools. On the floor, directly in front of each of them, lay two shilling pieces. Outside the moon kept a straight face.

'We believe every word you say to be true', said Ezenwa. 'We shall, every one of us, drop our paper for Marcus. Who would leave an *ozo* feast and go to a poor ritual meal? Tell Marcus he has our papers, and our wives' papers too. But what we do say is that two shillings is shameful.' He brought the lamp close and tilted it at the money before him as if to make sure he had not mistaken its value. 'Yes, two shillings is too shameful. If Marcus were a poor man – which our ancestors forbid – I should be the first to give him my paper free, as I did before. But today Marcus is a great man and does his things like a great man. We did not ask him for money yesterday; we shall not ask him tomorrow. But today is our day; we have climbed the iroko tree today and would be foolish not to take down all the firewood we need.'

Roof had to agree. He had lately been taking down a lot of firewood himself. Only yesterday he had asked Marcus for one of his many rich robes, and had got it. Last Sunday Marcus's wife (the teacher that nearly got him in trouble) had objected (like the woman she was) when Roof pulled out his fifth bottle of beer from the kerosene refrigerator; she was roundly and publicly rebuked by her husband. To cap it all Roof had won a land case recently because, among other things, he had been chauffeur-driven to the disputed site. So he understood the elders about the firewood.

'All right,' he said in English and then reverted to Ibo. 'Let us not quarrel about small things.' He stood up and adjusted his robes. Then he bent down like a priest distributing the host and gave one shilling more to every man; only he did not put it into their palms but on the floor in front of them. The men, who had so far not deigned to touch the things, looked at the floor and shook their heads. Roof got up again and gave each man another shilling.

'I am through,' he said with a defiance that was no less effective for being transparently faked. The elders too knew how far to go without losing decorum. So when Roof added: 'Go cast your paper for the enemy if you like!' they quickly calmed him down with a suitable speech from each of them. By the time the last man had spoken it was possible, without great loss of dignity, to pick up the things from the floor.

The enemy Roof had referred to was the Progressive Organization Party (POP) which had been formed by the tribes down the coast to save themselves, as the founders of the party proclaimed, from 'total political, cultural, social and religious annihilation'. Although it was clear the party had no chance here it had plunged, with typical foolishness, into a straight fight with PAP, providing cars and loud-speakers to a few local rascals and thugs to go around and make a lot of noise. No one knew for certain how much money POP had let loose in Umuofia but it was said to be very considerable. Their local campaigners would end up very rich, no doubt.

Up to last night everything had been 'moving according to plan', as Roof would have put it. Then he had received a strange visit from the leader of the POP campaign team. Although he and Roof were well known to each other, and might even be called friends, his visit was cold and businesslike. No words were wasted. He placed five pounds on the floor before Roof and said, 'We want your vote.' Roof got up from his chair, went to the outside door, closed it carefully and returned to his chair. The brief exercise gave him enough time to weigh the proposition. As he spoke his eyes never left the red notes on the floor. He seemed to be mesmerized by the picture of the cocoa farmer harvesting his crops.

'You know I work for Marcus,' he said feebly. 'It will be very bad —'

'Marcus will not be there when you put in your paper. We have plenty of work to do tonight; are you taking this or not?'

'It will not be heard outside this room?' asked Roof.

'We are after votes not gossip.'

'All right,' said Roof in English.

The man nudged his companion and he brought forward an object covered with a red cloth and proceeded to remove the cover. It was a fearsome little affair contained in a clay pot with feathers stuck into it.

'This *iyi* comes from Mbanta. You know what that means. Swear that you will vote for Maduka. If you fail to do so, this *iyi* take note.'

Roof's heart nearly flew out when he saw the *iyi;* indeed he knew the fame of Mbanta in these things. But he was a man of quick decision. What could a single vote cast in secret for Maduka take away from Marcus's certain victory? Nothing.

'I will cast my paper for Maduka; if not this *iyi* take note.'

'Das all,' said the man as he rose with his companion who had covered up the object again and was taking it back to their car.

'You know he has no chance against Marcus,' said Roof at the door.

'It is enough that he gets a few votes now; next time he will get more. People will hear that he gives out pounds, not shillings, and they will listen.'

*   *   *

Election morning. The great day every five years when the people exercised power, or thought they did. Weather-beaten posters on walls of houses, tree-trunks and telegraph poles. The few that were still whole called out their message to those who could read. Vote for the People's Alliance Party! Vote for the Progressive Organization Party! Vote for P A P! Vote for P O P!

The posters that were torn called out as much of the message as they could.

As usual Chief the Honourable Marcus Ibe was doing things in grand style. He had hired a highlife band from Umuru and stationed it at such a distance from the voting booths as just managed to be lawful. Many villagers danced to the music, their ballot papers held aloft, before proceeding to the booths. Chief the Honourable Marcus Ibe sat in the 'owner's corner' of his enormous green car and smiled and nodded. One enlightened villager came up to the car, shook hands with the great man and said in advance; 'Congrats!' This immediately set the pattern. Hundreds of admirers shook Marcus's hand and said 'Corngrass!'

Roof and the other organizers were prancing up and down, giving last minute advice to the voters and pouring with sweat.

'Do not forget,' he said again to a group of illiterate women who seemed ready to burst with enthusiasm and good humour, 'our sign is the motor-car. . . .'

'Like the one Marcus is sitting inside.'

'Thank you, mother,' said Roof. 'It is the same car. The box with the car shown on its body is the box for you. Don't look at the other with the man's head: it is for those whose heads are not correct.'

This was greeted with loud laughter. Roof cast a quick and busy-like glance towards the Minister and received a smile of appreciation.

'Vote for the car,' he shouted, all the veins in his neck standing out. 'Vote for the car and you will ride in it!'

'Or if we don't our children will,' piped the same sharp, old girl.

The band struck up a new number: 'Why walk when you can ride. . . .'

In spite of his apparent calm and confidence Chief the Honourable Marcus was a relentless stickler for detail. He knew he would win what the newspapers called 'a landslide victory' but he did not wish, even so, to throw away a single vote. So as soon as the first rush of voters was over he promptly asked his campaign boys to go one at a time and put in their ballot papers.

'Roof, you had better go first,' he said.

Roof's spirits fell; but he let no one see it. All morning he had masked his deep worry with a surface exertion which was unusual even for him. Now he dashed off in his springy fashion towards the booths. A policeman at the entrance searched him for illegal ballot papers and passed him. Then the electoral officer explained to him about the two boxes. By this time the spring had gone clean out of his walk. He sidled in and was confronted by the car and the head. He brought out his ballot paper from his pocket and looked at it. How could he betray Marcus even in secret? He resolved to go back to the other man and return his five pounds. . . . Five pounds! He knew at once it was impossible. He had sworn on that *iyi*. The notes were red; the cocoa farmer busy at work.

At this point he heard the muffled voice of the policeman asking the electoral officer what the man was doing inside. 'Abi na pickin im de born?'

Quick as lighting a thought leapt into Roof's mind. He folded the paper, tore it in two along the crease and put one half in each box. He took the precaution of putting the first half into Maduka's box and confirming the action verbally: 'I vote for Maduka.'

They marked his thumb with indelible purple ink to prevent his return, and he went out of the booth as jauntily as he had gone in.

 People

Uncle Ben's 🌸 CHINUA ACHEBE
Choice

In the year nineteen hundred and nineteen I was a young clerk
in the Niger Company at Umuru. To be a clerk in those days is
like to be a Minister today. My salary was two pounds ten. You
may laugh but two pounds ten in those days is like fifty pounds
today. You could buy a big goat with four shillings. I could
remember the most senior African in the Company was one
Saro man on ten-thirteen-Four. He was like Governor-General
in our eyes.

Like all progressive young men I joined the African Club.
We played tennis and billiards. Every year we played a tourna-
ment with the European Club. But I was less concerned with
that. What I liked was the Saturday night dances. Women were
surplus. Not all the waw-waw women you see in townships
today but beautiful things like this.

I had a Raleigh bicycle, brand new, and everybody called me
Jolly Ben. I was selling like hot bread. But there is one thing
about me – we can laugh and joke and drink and do otherwise but
I must always keep my sense with me. My father told me that a
true son of our land must know how to sleep and keep one eye
open. I never forget it. So I played and laughed with everyone
and they shouted Jolly Ben! Jolly Ben! but I knew what I was
doing. The women of Umuru are very sharp; before you count
A they count B. So I had to be very very careful. I never showed
any of them the road to my house and I never ate the food they
cooked for fear of love potions. I had seen many young men
destroy themselves in those days, so I remembered my father's
word: Never let a handshake pass the elbow.

I can say that the only exception was one fair salt-water girl called Margaret. One Sunday morning like this I was playing my new gramophone – a brand new HMV Senior. (I never believe in second-hand things. If I have no money for a new one I just keep myself quiet.) I was playing this record and standing at the window with my chewing stick. People were passing in their fine-fine dresses to one church near my house. This Margaret was going with them when she saw me. As luck would have it I did not see her in time to hide. So that very day – she did not wait till tomorrow or next-tomorrow – but as soon as Church closed she returned back. According to her she wanted to convert me to Roman Catholic. Wonders will never end! Margaret Jumbo! But it is not Margaret I want to tell you about but how I stopped all that foolishness.

It was one New Year's Eve like this. You know how New Year can hot more than Christmas for salaried people. By Christmas Day the month has reached twenty-hungry but on New Year your pocket is heavy. So that day I went to the Club.

When I see you young men of nowadays say you drink I just laugh. You drink one bottle of beer or a shot of whisky and begin to holler like craze-people. That night I was taking it easy on White Horse. '*All that are desirous to pass from Edinburgh to London or any other place on their road, let them repair to the White Horse cellar . . .*' God Almighty!

One thing with me is I never mix my drinks. The day I want to drink whisky I call it whisky day; if I want to drink beer tomorrow then I don't touch any other thing. That night I was on White Horse. I had one roast chicken and a tin of Guinea Gold. Yes I used to smoke in those days. I only stopped when one German doctor told me my heart was as black as a cooking-pot. Those German doctors were spirits. You know they used to give injections in the head or belly or anywhere. You just point where the thing is paining you and they give it to you right there – they don't waste time.

What was I saying? . . . Yes, I drank a bottle of White Horse and put one roast chicken on top of it. . . . Drunk? It is not in

my dictionary. I have never been drunk in my life. My father used
to say that the cure for drink is to say no. When I want to drink I
drink, when I want to stop I stop. So about three o'clock that
night I jumped on my new Raleigh bicycle and went home
quietly to sleep.

At that time our Senior Clerk had just been jailed for stealing
bales of calico and I was acting in that capacity. So I lived in a
small Company house. You know where G.B. Olivant is today?
. . . Yes, overlooking the River Niger. This is where the house
was. I had two rooms on one side of it and the Store-keeper had
two rooms on the other side. But as luck would have it this man
was on leave, so his side was empty.

I opened the front door and went inside. Then I locked it again.
I left my bicycle in the first room and went into the bed-room. I
was too tired to begin to look for my lamp. So I pulled off my
dress and packed them on the back of a chair, and fell like a log
into my big iron bed. And fell on someone. My mind told me at
once it was Margaret. So I began to laugh and touch her here and
there. She was hundred per cent naked. I continued laughing and
asked her when did she come. She did not say anything and I
suspected she was annoyed because she asked me to take her to
the Club that day and I said no. I said to her: if you come there
we will meet, I don't take anybody to the Club as such. So I
suspected that is what is making her vex.

I told her not to vex but still she did not say anything. I asked
her if she was asleep – just for asking sake. She said nothing.
Although I told you that I did not like women to come to my
house, but for every rule there must be an exception. So if I say I
was angry to find Margaret that night I will be telling a white lie.
I was still laughing when I noticed that her breasts were like the
breasts of a girl of sixteen – or seventeen, at most. I thought that
perhaps it was because of the way she was lying on her back. But
when I touched her hair and it was soft like the hair of a European
my laughter quenched. I touched the hair on her head and it was
the same. I jumped out of the bed and shouted: Who are you?

My head swelled up like a barrel and I was shaking. The woman sat up and stretched her hands to call me back; as she did so her fingers touched me. I sprang back at the same time and shouted again to her to call her name. Then I said to myself: How can you be afraid of a woman? Whether a white woman or a black woman, it is the same ten and ten pence. So I said: All right, I will soon open your mouth; at the same time I began to look for matches on the table. The woman seemed to know what I was looking for. She said: 'Biko, akpakwana oku.'

I said: 'So you are not a white woman. Who are you? I will strike the light now if you don't tell me.' I shook the matches to show her I meant business. My boldness had come back and I was trying to remember the voice because it was very familiar.

'Come back to the bed and I will tell you,' was what I heard next. Whoever told me I knew that voice told me a lie. It was sweet like sugar but very strange. So I struck the match.

'I beg you,' was the last thing she said.

If I say what I did next or how I got out of the room it is pure guess-work. The next thing I remember is that I was running like a craze-man to Matthew's house. Then I was banging on his door with both hands.

'Who is that?' he said from inside.

'Open,' I shouted. 'In the name of God above, open.' I called my name but my voice was not like my voice. The door opened small and I saw my kinsman holding a matchet in his right hand.

I fell down on the floor, and he said, 'God will not agree.'

It was God Himself who directed me to Matthew Obi's house that night because I did not see where I was running. I could not say whether I was still in this world or in the next one. Matthew poured cold water on me and after a while I was able to tell him what happened. I think I told it upside-down otherwise he would not keep asking me what was she like.

'I told you before I did not see her,' I said.

'I see, but you heard her voice?'

'I heard her voice quite all right. And I touched her and she touched me.'

'I don't know whether you did well or not to scare her away,' was what Matthew said.

I don't know how to explain it but those words from Matthew opened my eyes. I knew then that I had been visited by Mami Wota, the Lady of the River Niger.

Matthew said again: 'It depends what you want in life. If it is wealth you want then you made a great mistake today, but if you are a true son of your father then take my hand.'

We shook hands and he said: 'Our fathers never told us that a man should prefer wealth instead of wives and children.'

Today whenever my wives make me vex I tell them: I don't blame you. If I had been wise I would have taken Mami Wota. They laugh and ask me why did I not take her. The youngest one says: 'Don't worry, Papa, she will come again, she will come tomorrow.' And they laugh again.

But we all know it is a joke. For where is the man who will choose wealth instead of children? Except a crazy white man like Dr. S. M. Stuart-Hill. Oh, I didn't tell you. The same night that I drove Mami Wota out she went to Dr. S. M. Stuart-Hill, a white merchant and became his lover. You have heard of him? ... Oh yes, he became the richest man in the whole country. But she did not allow him to marry. When he died, what happened? All his wealth went to outsiders. Is that good wealth? I ask you. God forbid.

Certain Winds 🏵 AMA ATA AIDOO
from the South

M'ma Asana eyed the wretched pile of cola-nuts, spat, and picked up the reed-bowl. Then she put down the bowl, picked up one of the nuts, bit at it, threw it back, spat again, and stood up. First, a sharp little ache, just a sharp little one, shot up from somewhere under her left ear. Then her eyes became misty.

'I must check on those logs,' she thought, thinking this misting of her eyes was due to the chill in the air. She stooped over the nuts.

'You never know what evil eyes are prowling this dust over these grasslands, I must pick them up quickly.'

On the way back to the kraal her eyes fell on the especially patchy circles that marked where the old pits had been. At this time, in the old days, they would have been nearly bursting and as one scratched out the remains of the out-going season, one felt a near-sexual thrill of pleasure looking at these pits, just as one imagines a man might feel who looks upon his wife in the ninth month of pregnancy.

Pregnancy and birth and death and pain; and death again . . . when there are no more pregnancies, there are no more births, and therefore, no more deaths. But there is only one death and only one pain.

Show me a fresh corpse, my sister, so I can weep you old tears.

The pit of her belly went cold, then her womb moved and she had to lean by the doorway. In twenty years Fuseni's has been the only pregnancy and the only birth. Twenty years, and the first child and a male! In the old days, there would have been bucks and you got scolded for serving a woman in maternity a duicker.

But these days those mean poachers on the government reserves sneak away their miserable duickers, such wretched hinds! Yes they sneak away even the duickers to the houses of those sweet-toothed southerners.

In the old days, how time goes, and how quickly age comes. But then does one expect to grow younger when one starts getting grandchildren? Allah be praised for a grandson.

The fire was still strong when she returned to the room. M'ma Asana put the nuts down. She craned her neck into the corner. At least those logs should take them to the following week. For the rest of the evening, she sat about preparing for the morrow's marketing.

The evening prayers were done. The money was in the bag. The grassland was still, Hawa was sleeping and so was Fuseni. M'ma came out to the main gate, first to check up if all was well outside and then to draw the door across. It was not the figure, but rather the soft rustle of light footsteps trying to move still more lightly over the grass, that caught her attention.

'If only it could be my husband.'

But of course it was not her husband!

'Who comes?'

'It is me, M'ma.'

'You Issa, my son?'

'Yes, M'ma.'

'They are asleep.'

'I thought so. That is why I am coming now.'

There was a long pause in the conversation as they both hesitated about whether the son-in-law should go in to see Hawa and the baby or not. Nothing was said about this struggle but then one does not say everything.

M'ma Asana did not see but felt him win the battle. She crossed the threshold outside and drew the door behind her. Issa led the way. They did not walk far, however. They just turned into a corner between two of the projecting pillars in the wall of the

Kraal. It was as it should have been for it was he who needed the comforting coolness of it for his backbone.

'M'ma, is Fuseni well?'

'Yes.'

'M'ma, is Hawa well?'

'Yes.'

'M'ma please tell me, is Fuseni very well?'

'A-ah, my son. For what are you troubling yourself so much? Fuseni is a new baby who was born not more than ten days ago. How can I tell you he is very well? When a grown-up goes to live in other people's village . . .'

'M'ma?'

'What is it?'

'No. Please, it is nothing.'

'My son, I cannot understand you this evening. . . . yes, if you, a grown-up person, go to live in another village, will you say after the first few days that you are perfectly well?'

'No.'

'Shall you not get yourself used to their food? Shall you not find first where you can get water for yourself and your sheep?'

'Yes, M'ma.'

'Then how is it you ask me if Fuseni is very well? The navel is healing very fast . . . and how would it not? Not a single navel of all that I have cut here got infected. Shall I now cut my grandson's and then sit and see it rot? But it is his male that I can't say. Mallam did it neat and proper and it must be all right. Your family is not noted for males that rot, is it now?'

'No, M'ma.'

'Then let your heart lie quiet in your breast. Fuseni is well but we cannot say how well yet.'

'I have heard you, M'ma. M'ma?'

'Yes, my son.'

'M'ma, I am going south.'

'Where did you say?'

'South.'

'How far?'

'As far as the sea. M'ma, I thought you would understand.'

'Have I spoken yet?'

'No, you have not.'

'Then why did you say that?'

'That was not well said.'

'And what are you going to do there?'

'Find some work.'

'What work?'

'I do not know.'

'Yes you know, you are going to cut grass.'

'Perhaps.'

'But my son, why must you travel that far just to cut grass? Is there not enough of it all round here? Around this kraal, your father's and all the others in the village? Why do you not cut these?'

'M'ma, you know it is not the same. If I did that here people would think I was mad. But over there, I have heard that not only do they like it but the government pays you to do it.'

'Even so, our men do not go south to cut grass. This is for those further north. They of the wilderness, it is they who go south to cut grass. This is not for our men.'

'Please M'ma, already time is going. Hawa is a new mother and Fuseni my first child.'

'And yet you are leaving them to go south and cut grass.'

'But M'ma, what will be the use in my staying here and watching them starve? You yourself know that all the cola went bad, and even if they had not, with trade as it is, how much money do you think I would have got from them? And that is why I am going. Trade is broken and since we do not know when things will be good again, I think it will be better for me to go away.'

'Does Hawa know?'

'No, she does not.'

'Are you coming to wake her up at this late hour to tell her?'

'No.'

'You are wise.'

'M'ma, I have left everything in the hands of Amadu. He will come and see Hawa tomorrow.'

'Good.'

'When shall we expect you back?'

'Issa.'

'M'ma.'

'When shall we expect you back?'

'M'ma, I do not know. Perhaps next Ramaddan.'

'Good.'

'So I go now.'

'Allah go with you.'

'And may His prophet look after you all.'

M'ma went straight back to bed, but not to sleep. And how could she sleep? At dawn, her eyes were still wide open.

'Is his family noted for males that rot? No, certainly not. It is us who are noted for our unlucky females. There must be something wrong with them . . . Or how is it we cannot hold our men? Allah, how is it?'

'Twenty years ago. Twenty years, perhaps more than twenty years . . . perhaps more than twenty years and Allah, please, give me strength to tell Hawa.

'Or shall I go to the market now and then tell her when I come back? No. Hawa, Hawa, now look at how you are stretched down there like a log! Does a mother sleep like this? Hawa, H-a-a-w-a! Oh, I shall not leave you alone . . . and how can you hear your baby when it cries in the night since you die when you sleep?

'Listen to her asking me questions! Yes, it is broad daylight. I thought you really were dead. If it is cold, draw your blanket round you and listen to me for I have something to tell you.

'Hawa, Issa has gone south.

'And why do you stare at me with such shining eyes. I am telling you that Issa is gone south.

'And what question do you think you are asking me? How could he take you along when you have a baby whose navel wound has not even healed yet?

'He went away last night.

'Don't ask me why I did not come and wake you up. What should I have woken you up for? Listen, Issa said he could not stay here and just watch you and Fuseni starve.

'He is going south to find work, and . . . Hawa, where do you think you are getting up to go? Issa is not at the door waiting for you. The whole neighbourhood is not up yet, so do not let me shout . . . and why are you behaving like a baby? Now you are a mother and you must decide to grow up . . . where are you getting up to go? Listen to me telling you this. Issa is gone. He went last night because he wants to catch the government bus that leaves Tamale very early in the morning. So . . .

'Hawa, ah-ah, are you crying? Why are you crying? That your husband has left you to go and work? Go on weeping, for he will bring the money to look after me and not you . . .

'I do not understand, you say? Maybe I do not . . . See, now you have woken up Fuseni. Sit down and feed him and listen to me.

'Listen to me and I will tell you of another man who left his newborn child and went away.

'Did he come back? No, he did not come back. But do not ask me any more questions for I will tell you all.

'He used to go and come, then one day he went away and never came back. Not that he had to go like the rest of them . . .

'Oh, they were soldiers. I am talking of a soldier. He need not have gone to be a soldier. After all, his father was one of the richest men of this land. He was not the eldest son, that is true, but still there were so many things he could have done to look after himself and his wife when he came to marry. But he would not listen to anybody. How could he sit by and have other boys out-do him in smartness?

'Their clothes that shone and shone with pressing . . . I say, you could have looked into any of them and put khole under your eyes. And their shoes, how they roared! You know soldiers for yourself. Oh, the stir on the land when they came in from the south! Mothers spoke hard and long to daughters about the excellencies of proper marriages, while fathers hurried through with betrothals. Most of them were afraid of getting a case like that of Memunat on their hands. Her father had taken the cattle and everything and then Memunat goes and plays with a soldier. Oh, the scandal she caused herself then!

'Who was this Memunat? No, she is not your friend's mother. No, this Memunat in the end ran away south herself. We hear she became a bad woman in the city and made a lot of money.

'No, we do not hear of her now. She is not dead either, for we hear such women usually go to their homes to die, and she has not come back here yet.

'But us, we were different. I had not been betrothed.

'Do you ask me why I say "we"? Because this man was your father. Ah-ah, you open your mouth and eyes wide? Yes, my child, it is of your father I am speaking.

'No, I was not lying when I told you that he died. But keep quiet and listen. He was going south to get himself a house for married soldiers.

'No, it was not that time he did not come back. He came here, but not to fetch me.

'He asked us if we had heard of the war.

'Had we not heard of the war? Was it not difficult to get things like tinned fish, kerosene and cloth?

'Yes, we said, but we thought it was only because the traders were not bringing them in.

'Well yes, he said, but the traders do not get them even in the south.

'And why, we asked.

'Oh you people, have you not heard of the German people? He had no patience with us. He told us that in the south they were singing dirty songs with their name.

'But when are we going, I asked him?

'What he told me was that, that was why he had come. He could not take me along with him. You see, he said we were under the Anglis-people's rule and they were fighting with the German-people.

'Ask me, my child, for that was exactly what I asked him. What has all that got to do with you and me? Why can I not come south with you?'

'Because I have to travel to the lands beyond the sea and fight.

'In other people's war? My child, it is as if you were there, that is what I asked him.

'But it is not as simple as that, he said.

'We could not understand him. You shall not go, said his father. You shall not go, for it is not us fighting with the Grunshies or the Gonjas.

'I know about the Anglis-people but not about any German-people, but anyway they are in their country.

'Of course his father was playing, and so was I.

'A soldier must obey at all times, he said.

'I wanted to give him so many things to take with him but he said he could only take cola.

'Then the news came. It did not enter my head, for it was all empty. Everything went into my womb. You were just three days old.

'The news was like fore which settled in the pit of my belly. And from time to time, some will shoot up, searing my womb, singeing my intestines and burning up and up and up until I screamed with madness when it got into my head.

'I had told myself when you were born that it did not matter you were a girl. All gifts from Allah are good and anyway he was coming back and we were going to have many more children, lots of sons.

'But Hawa, you had a lot of strength, for how you managed to live I do not know. Three days you were and suddenly like a rivulet that is hit by an early harmattan, my breasts went dry. Hawa, you have a lot of strength.

'Later, they told me that if I could go south and prove to the government's people that I was his wife I would get a lot of money.

'But I did not go. It was him I wanted not his body turned into gold.

'I never saw the south.

'Do you say "oh"? My child I am always telling you that the world was created a long while ago and it is old-age one has seen but not youth. So do not say "oh".

'Those people, the government's people, who came and go, tell us trade is bad now, and once again there is no tinned fish and no cloth. But this time they say this is because our children are going to get them in abundance one day.

'Issa has gone south now because he cannot afford even goat flesh for his wife in maternity. This has to be, so that Fuseni can stay with his wife and eat cow-meat with her? Hmm. And he will come back alive . . . perhaps not next Ramaddan but the next. Now my daugher, you know of another man who went to fight. And he went to fight in other people's war and he never came back.

'I am going to the market now. Get up early to wash Fuseni. I hope to get something for those miserable colas. There is enough rice for two, is there not?

'Good. Today even if it takes all the money, I hope to get us some smoked fish, the biggest I can find, to make us a real good sauce.'

Constable ✿ O. R. DATHORNE

I remember I was in Kano a few years ago. It was a Saturday evening, Harmattan season, and I decided I would have a bite at the National and then go home for a much-needed rest. I was destined not to get home that night and my much-needed rest was delayed for another twenty-four hours. This was because of Constable.

I requested African fare at the African-owned National and was abruptly led out of the plush dining-room where courteous waiters anticipated your every need. I was led through a passage-way into a dark interior where on roughly hewn tables food was dished up into enamel plates. The spruce waiter said, 'Na here for African chop.' It sounded like a punishment. I sat down and was half-way through my *fu-fu* when several things made themselves felt at the same time. The first was that the clawing motion which I employ when I am eating *fu-fu* was impeded by the presence of a huge enormous hat which obstructed the movement of my hand from *fu-fu* to soup. This hat was of a peculiar Existentialist construction and had a huge and enormous hat-band. On looking up to detect the reason for the interference – eating and I are first cousins and interruption is sacrilegious – on looking up, I perceived, or rather heard, Constable. Constable's fingers went into his pounded yam like a road-builder's tractor and emerged full to capacity. The movement which he employed to dip his hand in his stew was equally swift and sure and the speed and precision with which his hands found his ever-masticating jaws was equally incredible. Not once did he cease in this steady movement of hand and mouth, not once did the rotation of jaws cease, not once did the large, sucking noise subside.

I have known Constable now for some years and not once have I ever ceased to be fascinated by his table manners. It was not merely that Constable ate like a pig; it was that at table Constable gave up all claims to being human and became a swine. The third and most miraculous thing of all was that all the time the hat was manœuvring and the giant prongs of fingers were shovelling yam into his guzzle, Constable kept up a flow of conversation, made all the more ridiculous because it verged on the inane. 'Is blowing today – cay! This Harmattan weather go kill man.' Or in a burst of political frenzy – 'Wha' kin gov'ment be this we get – they no dey know some o' we no dey even get money to chop.' These were Constable's three main topics of conversation in inverted order – the growing cost of eating, the gov'ment, and the weather.

Somehow in between these activities he introduced himself, 'I am a policeman', and then he beat his breast and shovelled the food faster down and spat across the table into another diner's lap and cursed the waiter for the umpteenth time.

'I am a policeman,' Constable bellowed and the table shook. Reluctant diners gave their unfinished food a hasty look and departed. The Proprietor nervously wiped clean glasses with a dirty rag. Kano waited.

Constable said to me, 'Make we leave the National. I go take you for the Renvous-dez.' We left the National. One usually did what Constable said, willingly or unwillingly. The National saw us go. An indecisive diner on his way back in to finish the dregs of his meal was halted by Constable. 'Wa'ting you dey go for?'

'No – no – ting, Sah,' the customer stammered.

Constable slapped him on his back and laughed. He bellowed to the Kano skies. 'I am a policeman.' The man ran outside, jumped on his bicycle and was off. Before we walked away, Constable pushed down all the cycles outside by touching the saddle of the outermost one with a gentle, surgical precision. There was a clattering of machinery, spokes and a fan-fare of

bells. Owners rushed out. Constable bellowed 'I am a policeman.'

We went through the streets while Constable conversed.
Occasionally he broke off, abruptly, to proclaim his identity to
the empty street, taking care to state his vocation. People who
saw him were perhaps unkind enough to think him drunk but
this was far from the case. I have never known Constable any
different. Either he had attained a state of permanent alcoholism
or he had managed to attain a delicate balance between sobriety
and intoxication and explored the narrow frontiers of his own
no-man's land. At the 'Ren-vous-dez', he forgot all about me,
soundly cursed the gateman and passed in free. Then the little
voice of Conscience must have whispered to him as he got in, for
I heard again the glad tidings as he proclaimed his re-appearance.
Meantime I was being eyed very suspiciously by the official
'chuck-him-out' and the smaller, more delicate money collector.
'Hey!' The money-collector spoke to thin air. 'Some people
t'ink they go pass in for free. Ha!' The 'chuck-him-out' flexed his
muscles and yawned anticipatively. Then Constable re-appeared.

'A very good friend,' Constable said, digressing slightly from
his normal conversational topics. The money-collector shifted
uncomfortably. The 'chuck-him-out' gazed abstractedly into the
distant point of nothing with deaf concentration.

'Eh! Eh!' Constable digressed further. 'These man is the Headmaster of the University of Lagos.'

The 'chuck-him-out' was hard of hearing. The money-
collector said, 'Is all right for you to go in free, Constable, but
these man must pay.' Constable bellowed to the skies, 'I am a
policeman.' Kano shook with fright. Two girls paid their
entrance-fee and passed in giggling nervously. Then abruptly
Constable departed again.

I was left outside. The Harmattan blew cold air up the legs of
my trousers and explored my person. I started to shiver. 'Warmer
inside,' the money-collector said helpfully. 'Even fire dey. No be
so ?' he asked the 'chuck-him-out'. The abstractionist returned to

earth, reflexed his tired muscles, grunted and turned his back. His shirt had 'Killer, captain, killer, captain' written monotonously all over it, as if the designer had been inspired by some idea to re-create a Hercules. 'I am a policeman' a voice bellowed from the inside and Constable appeared, drink in hand. The 'chuck-him-out' once more became abstract; the money-collector forgot his meteorological observations to me. Constable said, 'You don't really t'ink these man is the Headmaster of the University of Lagos?'

The 'chuck-him-out' almost defrosted and allowed the thin hint of a smile to wet the corners of his frozen features. The talkative money collector grew exuberant, 'Heh! Heh! Heh!' he bellowed in empty mirthless laughter. 'We known na joke you make. Headmaster of University no be anything to us.' 'These man,' Constable pronounced, 'is travellin' incognito – that mean say – he no want anybody know who he is.'

The milk of human kindness started to flow through the 'chuck-him-out's' veins; he started hearing in one ear. 'Na who?' he asked, curiosity changing him over from a dreamy abstractionist into an eager quester.

'I am a policeman,' Constable bellowed relevantly, 'and these man is the owner of the Commonwealth Hotel in Kaduna.'

'The owner —?' The money collector was stuck for words, wonder and admiration getting the better of him.

'Make'e pass,' the 'chuck-him-out' said slowly and distinctly. He had now begun to hear in both ears and had become completely human. 'Sorry, sir,' he said to me. 'I never know.'

The money collector stood up, touched his cap and bowed.

'Welcome, sir' he said.

'I am a policeman' Constable shouted across the floor.

The Bark ❀ BISHR FARES

TRANSLATED BY
ULLI BEIER

The sun visits those who desire him. The room has four windows. All four are wide open and the room remains dark: the lung of a consumptive, inhaling air, yet unable to expand.

Furniture is lined up in the room, ready to fly away when it is touched. It is intended for a tribe of wandering angels? There is a rare little statue here, that was finished only after it had buried three Chinese carvers in succession. There are also carpets here, that would fetch so much money if sold in North America that one could bribe the deputies of a highly developed country with it.

A dark room with four windows all wide open, wonderful objects ... and a man who never dared to ask himself why he was alive.

Suddenly the door was opened. Something penetrated that is divided into two colours, white and brown. One could say an autumn day, hesitating between rain and sunshine. Something that moves slowly: the hand of a painter, formulating an idea.

Something entered. The white spread out into all the corners of the room, illuminated them, while the brown went straight to the windows. Then the sun was led into the room.

The door had opened for a young girl, Amina.

'Are you coming to me with empty hands?'

'Forgive me, my friend, I have not finished the jumper; only one sleeve remains. I had hardly reached my house last night when I started work, but I was interrupted by the visit of a girl friend. And this morning I had to go out. My father had given me all kinds of commissions.'

'Very well, very well! Visits in the evening and outings in the morning. And yet you know that I am waiting impatiently for that jumper. And I told you that I was going to drive into the desert tomorrow morning at nine o'clock, with a few friends. Had I not explained to you that I wanted to put on sporty clothes and therefore needed the jumper? Moreover, I'd already told my friends about it. What will they be thinking, when it does not adorn my chest? Do you want me to become their laughing-stock? Why this silence. . . . ? Because you have lied to me. How pale your face is. Your eyelids seem to have fought each other all night refusing to come together. Listen! Did I perhaps ask you to knit this jumper? You wanted to give it to me. You said to me: "You will see how skilful I am, and if I am not, I will try to become skilful for the love of you. You will wear a jumper that will have no equal. My eyes, watching my fingers, will com-municate a gay freshness to it." All that is just poetry, my dear. But the jumper, the concrete object, where is it? You turn your head away. Well, that's better.'

On the Nile, of which one sees neither the beginning nor the end. Here one can breathe more freely; no danger of suffocating.

Amina leant on a wall at the riverbank. The dams were not built for Amina; nothing can flood her. She is overflowing her-self. She was created to spread out, to overflow. Amina is a second Nile.

The bridge suddenly divided into two parts in order to let a sailing bark pass. Since there was no wind the oars were at work, but very gently. One could have said the bark was asking per-mission from the water to glide along, or it apologized for dividing the water.

Amina asked the bark, 'Where are you going? What are you carrying? Honey or straw? Corn or perhaps dates? The journey has surely exhausted you. May he who is expecting you not receive the honey melted by the sun, the straw soaked in water, the corn eaten by beetles nor the dates soiled by dust! What is the use of your journey, if your load does not satisfy? He who is expecting you will not appreciate the hardships you endured but what could you have endured in gliding along like that? After all you are a bark. Do walls exhaust the warrior? Was he not born to fight? Oh bark, stop, stop, before you disappear from my sight . . . you disappear too fast, for I want to rest my eyes this night. Before you disappear, bark, I say this to you: it is harder to throw anchor than to sail . . . the bridge is still open. If there is danger that your load might disappoint, turn back. Fear the ignorance of the heart. Bark, turn back, turn back!'

'What have you been doing, Amina? Your defeat is written on your face.'

'Defeat? You are right, father.'

'Whom did you talk to? What did you say to each other?'

'Early on I went to the same master. I apologized for not being able to keep my promise. I repeated the words to him, words that you my father had impressed upon me. I said that I could not bring this jumper because I had suddenly run out of wool, that this wool was rare, and that yesterday I tried in vain to get it. But he became angry and threatened and gave me a deadline. I must bring the jumper tomorrow morning before nine o'clock. I must submit, I must . . . I fear the competition. Who knows? Another girl could have more skilful fingers.'

'Do you think he will give us a few piasters? Or will he insist not to pay anything for the first work.'

'He will not give us anything, father.'

'And if you told him the truth?'

'Should I tell him then that I could not keep my word because we were without electric light, since we had not been able to pay the electric light bill and I could not knit in the dark? Should I tell him I was from eight in the morning till six in the evening with my aunt, that I look after her children and that she feeds both of us in return? Or should I tell him that you have lost your job? No, no, I cannot accept any alms from this man.'

'But these are not alms, Amina. And if they were alms, is this

man so mean that you should fear to arouse his pity? I should
like to meet him.'

'No father, no, you shall not meet him. I have no doubt that he
would have given us a pound, or even two, if I had explained our
position to him, but I did not dare to. Can I ask him to help me,
when he believes that our needs are provided for?'

'But they are not provided for.'

'But he believes it . . . or rather, I made him believe it. No. It is
impossible to accept even the smallest gift from this man. He
knows nothing about poverty. I cannot be responsible for
exposing the wounds to him.'

'Strange.'

'Oh, if only you knew . . .'

'If I knew what?'

'Have I said anything? Have I?'

'You said: if only you knew.'

'Then I have not said anything at all. Anyhow, I have nothing
to say.'

'So you will knit that sleeve tonight?'

'Yes.'

'And your eyes? I fear you will ruin them.'

'Fear nothing, father. I have been resting them since noon.
Since I let my eyes glide over the Nile: a little, just a little.'

'But with what light will you be knitting?'

'With the light of something that is burning here in my
breast.'

'You spoke so softly. I could not understand it.'

'I said: with the light of the moon . . . the moon is the friend of
those who live in darkness.'

The father sat down beside his daughter. Amina's fingers
began to move and the wool unravelled.

The father pressed the girl to his breast. 'Amina, do not leave
me. My love for you is like that of a husband. You are happy
with me. Would you be equally happy with a companion,
Amina? Why are your eyes suddenly moist? Are you beginning

to weep before the moon? Ah, Amina . . . Amina . . . I have expressed myself badly. Forgive me, with my words I was thinking only of myself.'

Amina replied, 'Can a man think of anything but himself?'

And her fingers began to move again.